rororo sprachen

Herausgegeben von [illegible]

[illegible]

[illegible]

rororo

rororo sprachen
Herausgegeben von Ludwig Moos

Some people just have it – manche haben's einfach drauf. Die Verständigung mit Engländern und Amerikanern gelingt mühelos, wenn Sie *Flüssiges Englisch* intus haben. Denn erst mit dem Verstehen und Gebrauchen bildhafter Idiome beginnt man, sich in der Fremdsprache frei zu bewegen. *Flüssiges Englisch* präsentiert die wichtigsten Redensarten und Wendungen gleich dreifach: im Kontext griffiger Dialoge und unterhaltsamer Kurzgeschichten, in lockeren Übungen zum Aneignen und systematisch verzeichnet zum gezielten Nachschlagen.

Nach dem gleichen Muster sind erschienen:
Flüssiges Französisch (rororo sprachen 61184), *Flüssiges Italienisch* (rororo sprachen 61185) und *Flüssiges Spanisch* (rororo sprachen 61186).

Uwe Kreisel / Pamela Ann Tabbert

Flüssiges Englisch

Mit Redensarten zu mehr Eloquenz

Illustrationen Mathias Hütter

Buchkonzept Christof Kehr

Rowohlt Taschenbuch Verlag

IMPRESSUM

Überarbeitete Neuausgabe August 2001

Veröffentlicht im Rowohlt Taschenbuch Verlag GmbH,
Reinbek bei Hamburg, Oktober 1994 unter dem Titel
Ultimate Idioms

Umschlaggestaltung und Illustration Britta Lembke

Layout Iris Christmann/Alexander Urban

Satz TimesTen und Futura PostScript,
QuarkXPress 4.0

Gesamtherstellung Clausen & Bosse, Leck

Printed in Germany

ISBN 3 499 61183 X

INHALT

VORWORT

Da hat man nun jahrelang Englisch gepaukt, beherrscht die Grammatik leidlich und versteht dann doch nur wenig, wenn Engländer oder Amerikaner loslegen. Das wirklich Schlimme ist, dass es am akustischen Verstehen nicht liegt: Die Ohren kriegen jedes Wort mit, aber nichts ergibt einen richtigen Sinn. Sätze wie «Charles flew off the handle» lassen einen nur ratlos mit den Schultern zucken. Was, fragt man sich, soll denn das bloß heißen? Mit einer wörtlichen Übersetzung lässt sich dem Idiom «to fly off the handle» offensichtlich nicht beikommen: «Charles flog vom Griff.» Erst im idiomatischen Wörterbuch löst sich das Rätsel. Gemeint ist, dass Charles fuchsteufelswild wurde.

Doch nicht nur beim Verstehen, auch beim Sprechen gibt es Probleme für phraseologisch Ungeschulte. Jeder, der wenigstens einmal im Ausland war, weiß, wie schnell man sich mit wörtlichen, unidiomatischen Übersetzungen in eine sprachliche Sackgasse reden kann. Selbst in einem Filmklassiker wie «Casablanca» wird das zum Thema: «What watch?», radebrecht der nach der Uhrzeit fragende österreichische Emigrant in *Rick's Café Américain*. Kaum hat er Antwort bekommen, macht er genauso falsch weiter, wie er begonnen hat: «What? Such much watch?» Aber auch Freunde idiomatisch korrekter Wendungen kommen in «Casablanca» auf ihre Kosten. Humphrey Bogarts «I stick my neck out for nobody» lässt sich um einiges leichter verstehen, sobald Sie aus dem «neck» einen «head» gemacht haben: «Ich halte für niemanden den Kopf hin.»

Für dieses Buch haben wir eine Menge gebräuchlicher Redewendungen gesammelt, die wir dann auf Alltagstauglichkeit abgeklopft haben. Aufgenommen wurde, was uns im Alltagsgespräch, in Film und Fernsehen, in der englischsprachigen Gegenwartsliteratur immer wieder begegnet ist. Aus den ursprünglich zweitausend gesammelten Redewendungen haben wir einen Grundstock von rund eintausend in den Anhang dieses Buches aufgenommen und mit deutschen Übersetzungen versehen («Idioms from A to Z»). Unter «Functions & Notions» bieten wir zusätzlich ein thematisches Verzeichnis aller Wendungen, ebenfalls mit deutscher Übersetzungshilfe. Es erleichtert die intuitive Suche nach dem passenden Idiom.

Nicht immer ließ sich eine so genaue Entsprechung finden wie für «to hit the nail on the head», den Nagel auf den Kopf treffen; in schwierigeren Fällen umschreiben wir deshalb die Bedeutung. Zuweilen liegt der Sinn eines englischen Idioms zwischen zwei deutschen Wendungen; beispielsweise entspricht «You can't teach an old dog new tricks» (Einem alten Hund kann man keine neuen Kunststückchen mehr beibringen) in etwa dem deutschen Sprichwort «Was Hänschen nicht lernt, lernt Hans nimmermehr», hat aber auch einen leichten Beigeschmack von «Einen alten Baum verpflanzt man nicht».

Zum *Lesen* und *Lernen* haben wir weitere achtzig besonders häufig auftretende Redewendungen nach Herkunftsbegriffen in acht Kategorien eingeteilt (Geld, Natur, Zeit ...) und haben dann für jedes dieser Idioms zwei kurze Szenen geschrieben, die es in einen eindeutigen Kontext stellen. Innerhalb eines Kapitels fügen sich jeweils die zehn Szenen mit ungeraden Nummern und die zehn Szenen mit geraden Nummern zu zwei abgeschlossenen Storys zusammen.

Bei der Lektüre schlagen wir vor, zuerst die ungeraden Szenen (1, 3, ... 19, obere Seitenhälfte) zu lesen, immer mit Blick auf das Vokabular. Um die Orientierung zu erleichtern, haben wir jeweils am unteren Seitenrand die Redewendung übersetzt, um die sich auf dieser Seite alles dreht, einmal sinngemäß und einmal – mit Klammern versehen – wortwörtlich. Man sehe uns das verschrobene Deutsch nach, das sich zwangsläufig einstellt, wenn man eine fremdsprachige Redewendung Wort für Wort übersetzt. Hier heiligt der didaktische Zweck, nämlich der einer humoristischen Eselsbrücke, die sprachlichen Mittel.

Hat man die ungeraden Szenen hinter sich, widmet man sich den übrigen Szenen (2, 4, ... 20, untere Hälfte), deren Lektüre dann schon ein Stück flotter vorangehen sollte, denn die Redewendung, in der am Ende alles gipfelt, ist ja schon aus der ersten Story bekannt. Wer an unbekannten

Wörtern oder Wendungen hängen bleibt, kann jeweils nach der zwanzigsten Szene (20, 40, ... 160) einen Blick auf «Vocabulary» werfen. Am Ende eines Kapitels finden sich die «Exercises»: vier Übungen, die das gerade Gelernte einschleifen helfen. Die Lösungen zu allen Übungen finden sich im Anhang unter «Answers».

Wem achtzig Idioms in sechzehn Storys noch immer nicht genug sind, der darf auf weitere 220 alltagssprachliche Wendungen gespannt sein, die wir zusätzlich mit in die Texte aufgenommen haben — freilich nicht, ohne sie im Vokabelteil wie auch im Anhang übersetzt zu haben.

Meist sind die Texte als Zwiegespräche angelegt, doch ab und an verlassen wir die Dialogform und machen hemmungslos Anleihen bei Schauergeschichten, Krimis, Liebesschnulzen und Cowboygroschenheften. Der Wortschatz stellt bei diesen Texten etwas höhere Anforderungen, schult aber zugleich für eigene Leseabenteuer. Mit Schulenglisch (*textbook English*) hat all das nichts mehr zu tun, es handelt sich um idiomatische Gegenwartssprache, die zuweilen auch das Fahrwasser traditioneller Grammatik verlässt.

Die aufgenommenen Idioms stammen aus den unterschiedlichsten Bereichen. Manches ist literarisch («The world is my oyster», Shakespeare, The Merry Wives of Windsor), manches geht auf kulturelle Eigenarten zurück: Wer in angelsächsischen Ländern auf gutes Gelingen hofft, sagt nicht «Drückt mir die Daumen!», sondern «Keep your fingers crossed!», haltet Zeige- und Mittelfinger gekreuzt, um mir Glück zu bringen. Wieder andere Idioms sind wohl als Scherzworte entstanden, dann aber in die Alltagssprache eingegangen, wie beispielsweise «not to have a snowball's chance in hell».

Entscheidend bei der Aufnahme in unsere Liste war immer die Frage, ob das entsprechende Idiom sowohl in den USA und Kanada als auch in Großbritannien und Australien gebräuchlich ist. Das gilt nicht nur für die gesprochene Alltagssprache, sondern auch für Alltagstexte: Was in den Printmedien auftaucht, sollte ebenso verstanden werden wie die Redewendung, mit der ein Muttersprachler seine Gespräche würzt. Dank schulden wir hier unseren Freunden aus Kanada (Ros Hiatt), Australien (Graham Stitz) und Großbritannien (Sue James), die alle in diesem Buch aufgeführten Idioms auf Verwendbarkeit in ihren Heimatländern überprüft und so unseren *American-English*-Horizont erweitert haben — was uns freilich nicht daran gehindert hat, hier durchweg die nervenschonende amerikanische Schreibweise zu benutzen.

Abschließend noch ein Rat: In der Bescheidung zeigt sich erst der Meister. Zu jeder passenden und unpassenden Gelegenheit ein Idiom ins Gespräch einzuflechten wirkt, besonders bei den eher redensartlichen, sentenziösen Wendungen, penetrant oder oft unfreiwillig komisch, vor allem wenn sie aus dem Mund eines Nicht-Muttersprachlers kommen. Hinzu kommt, dass man immer Gefahr läuft, ein lediglich halb verdautes Idiom im falschen Zusammenhang anzuwenden. Erst wer seiner Sache wirklich sicher ist, sollte den Sprung ins kalte Wasser wagen. Faustregel (englisch: *rule of thumb*, Daumenregel): Wenn Sie ein Idiom zehn- bis zwölfmal im Kontext gehört oder gelesen *und* verstanden haben, spricht nichts mehr gegen seine Benutzung. Nur Mut! Wer immer nur *textbook English* spricht, gilt bald als der größte Langweiler weit und breit. Wer das rechte Idiom im passenden Kontext beherrscht, signalisiert sprachliche Ebenbürtigkeit mit den Muttersprachlern, erzeugt Sympathie, ja sogar Bewunderung: «Talking to you is a real pleasure, you certainly have a way with words.»

TOPIC

1

ANIMAL KINGDOM

1

In the Wild West

A sky full of stars hung over the lonely prairie. All was quiet except for the occasional stamp of restless cattle or the howl of a coyote. Two tired cowboys lay near a blazing campfire.

«Sure is cold. Hey, Priest, you got any stories left to tell? I keep thinking about the end of this ride when I can crawl into a warm bed with my Mrs, and it's making me crazy. You got a woman waiting for you in town?»

«No.»

«Well, why not? Is that why folks call you Priest?»

«Well, Slim, sit back and I'll spin you a yarn that kills two birds with one stone. It'll answer your questions and take your mind off your wife.»

2

It's a jungle out there

The guy is really different. Lives here in the jungle with all the animals. Supposedly he can even talk to them. And all he wears is a loincloth.

Strange!

You can say that again.

What's his name?

Nobody really knows, but the natives call him «Tarzan the Ape Man».

Hey, why don't we check him out when take out the Landrover? That way we can kill two birds with one stone: Get some business done and find out who this mysterious Tarzan really is.

to kill two birds with one stone
zwei Fliegen mit einer Klappe schlagen
(zwei Vögel mit einem Stein töten)

!

3

Back East

The young man wrapped his rough blankets more tightly around his thin shoulders. Then he spoke.
«Okay, Priest, I'm listening. Shoot.»
«Well, Slim, it all started before you was even born, back East in Carolina. My father was a farmer there, an honest man with two sons. Me and my brother were like night and day. I was quiet and serious while my brother Jake was a reckless braggart always in trouble. One Sunday the most beautiful girl I'd ever seen walked into our lives. Golden curls and smooth white skin. Both Jake and I fell head over heels in love with Lilly. Jake was sure she'd marry him, but she chose me. That really ruffled Jake's feathers, so much so that he challenged me to a fight.»

4

Tarzan

I don't know. Maybe we should stay away from him. I'm getting a little nervous. What if he finds out about us?
He won't. He's too stupid. Did you hear him talk? He hardly spoke English. «Me Tarzan, you Jane.» Give me a break! Even my English is better than that, and I dropped out of school. The guy has the mind of a three-year-old.
I'm not so sure. That woman who lives with him...
Jane?
Yes, Jane. She wasn't too happy when we left. I think you ruffled her feathers when you told her we were here to catch animals for Taronga Zoo.

!

to ruffle someone's feathers
jemanden vergrätzen/verärgern
(jemandes Federn verwuscheln)

5 Right in the middle of town

Slim leaned forward, a glimmer of excitement in his eyes.
«So you fought your own brother. I bet you knocked the stuffing out of him.»
«That's where you're wrong, Slim. I couldn't raise a hand against my own flesh and blood. That made Jake even angrier. He cussed and cursed me right on Main Street with everybody watching and accused me of stealing Lilly just to prove I was better than him. When I calmly told him I wouldn't fight, he said my fiancée would be a widow before we even married.»
«He actually threatened to kill you?»
«I wasn't afraid. I knew he wouldn't really do it. His bark was always worse than his bite.»

6 After the rhinoceros hunt

I think we should move on and look for animals someplace else. This Tarzan fellow gives me the jitters. Last night when we caught those two rhinos, he was really upset. «You no touch Tarzan's animals — or else.» Lousy English, but I think he means business.
Ah, don't worry about him. He isn't going to do anything. The bloke is all talk. His bark is worse than his bite.

His bark is worse than his bite.
Hunde, die bellen, beißen nicht.
(Sein Bellen ist schlimmer als sein Beißen.)

!

7

Go West, Young Man

The listener poked at the embers of the dying fire and some sparks danced away on the wind.
«So what did you do?»
«I walked away and left him standing there in the street. After that I tried to avoid him, hoping he'd get over it and forgive me. But the pig-headed devil was deeply wounded. Whenever anybody mentioned me or Lilly or the wedding he'd start drinking and pick a fight. It was killing my mother. In the end I decided it would be best for me to leave town, to go West, so I wouldn't cause him any more pain. Sometimes it's better to let sleeping dogs lie.»

8

By the campfire

I wonder why we haven't seen Tarzan around lately?
Wherever he is, he probably misses us. Let's pay him a visit and remind him we're still here.
Forget it! He hasn't been breathing down our necks, watching us all the time, and I think that's just fine. I say we stay as far away from him and Jane as possible. Let sleeping dogs lie.

!

Let sleeping dogs lie.
Schlafende Hunde soll man nicht wecken. Rühre nicht an alte Geschichten.
(Lass schlafende Hunde liegen.)

9 An unknown land

The wind grew stronger, whistling through the boughs of the small tree they were camped under. Young Slim inched closer to the fire.
«You've had some bad luck, Priest.»
«The worst is yet to come. Back in those days, there weren't too many white men between here and there, just lots of Indians, buffalo and grass. My father was against it, he wanted me to stay and take over the farm. My mother was sure I'd be killed by Indians or die, sick with fever, thousands of miles from the nearest doctor. Their worries held me back, but in the end I couldn't wait any longer, my brother was getting worse, so I took the bull by the horns and left town.»

10 A murder plot

I've had it with this Tarzan bloke. It's time to get rid of him. Now that he's found out we're not really working for the zoo, he's making our lives miserable.
Jack, you're a man after my own heart. I'm fed up with him destroying our traps and chasing away all the animals. I'd love to pump Tarzan full of lead.
We can't just kill him off like that. We have to make it look like an accident. We need a plan.
Well, let's not waste too much time talking. It's best to take the bull by the horns and just do it.

!

to take the bull by the horns
den Stier bei den Hörnern packen
(den Stier bei den Hörnern nehmen)

11

In the wilderness

A coyote howled in the distance and made Slim shiver.

«And the girl? Surely, Lilly went with you.»

«No, it was too dangerous for a woman out in that wilderness. I wanted to make her a home before I brought her out, but everything went wrong. There was a drought, all my crops dried up, my animals died, I was just barely alive when the Indians came.

«The Indians? How did you get away from them?»

«Fool! The Indians saved me. They knew how to deal with the land, but I didn't. I almost died out there. That country put me through my paces, and I failed.»

12

The new car

Fantastic! This new Landrover is a beaut!

It better be, it wasn't cheap. We had to pay a lot of money for it, money we could've used for some new rifles, some ...

I know ... and I'm sorry. I should've been more careful with our old Landrover. But it wasn't my fault. I tried to run over Tarzan like we planned, but somehow he managed to jump into a tree. I stepped on the brakes, but it was too late.

No use crying over spilled milk. Let's put this baby through its paces and see what it can do.

!

to put one through one's paces

jemanden/etwas auf Herz und Nieren (seine Belastbarkeit) prüfen (jemanden/etwas durch alle Gangarten führen)

13 In St. Louis

Slim stretched his hands closer to the fire.
«What did you do, Priest?»
«I was sick and tired, so I headed East with some other discouraged souls to heal and prepare for another attempt. When I made it to St. Louis in the spring, a letter from my brother caught up with me. I wrote back, welcoming him again as my friend and relating all my troubles. I enclosed a letter for Lilly, writing I couldn't send for her until I was on my feet again — but I never had to send for her.»
«What? Why not?»
«That summer she married my brother. When I heard, I gave up my few remaining hopes and dreams and started wandering. That news was the straw that broke the camel's back.»

14 Another accident

I've had enough. I'm going home.
No, you're not. Calm down, mate, things can only get better. Cheer up.
Well, they can't get any worse than today. We've had rotten luck. First, we're almost eaten alive by crocodiles, and then an elephant wrecks our new Landrover. When Tarzan's monkey bit me, that was the straw that broke the camel's back. I want to go home.

the straw that broke the camel's back
der Tropfen, der das Fass zum Überlaufen brachte
(der Strohhalm, der dem Kamel das Rückgrat brach)

15

On the back of a horse

Slim didn't know what to say.

«Mighty sorry to hear that, Priest, but I don't understand.»

«Neither did I, Slim. That's why I went into mourning. I started wearing black and reading the Bible, looking for some answers. I wandered from ranch to ranch, earning my daily bread on the back of a horse. People started calling me Priest on account of my clothes and that Bible. And, of course, I never had anything to do with women. I was still in love with Lilly.»

«But why did she marry your brother?»

«I found out later the dirty scoundrel had tricked her. He never showed her my letter. Instead he told her a pretty nurse in St. Louis had stolen my heart. Lilly was devastated and finally agreed to marry him. She never learned the truth, never knew he was only crying wolf.»

16

Nerves of steel

That's it, we're done for, this is the end. We might as well pack up and get out of here.

Just because Tarzan and Jane said they would inform the police? Tarzan would never do that. He doesn't trust the police. He likes doing things his own way. He'd never cooperate with them.

Well, if that's true, why did they tell us they would talk to the police?

They were only crying wolf, so we'd get afraid and pack up.

!

to cry wolf

blinden Alarm schlagen; Alarm geben, um jemanden aufzurütteln

(«Wolf!» schreien)

17

At the Ponderosa

Slim tipped back his hat in astonishment.
«But how did you find out? Did she write?»
«No, I never heard from Lilly nor my brother again. They're both dead and buried now. I got older and stopped moving. I've made my home at the Ponderosa ranch for the past ten years. – She was happy, though. Had children.»
«Well, how can you be sure that's what happened?»
«Because I've heard it straight from the horse's mouth. A few years ago a fellow showed up at the ranch, and he told me what had happened. He was Jake and Lilly's son.»

18

A little money goes a long way

Are you sure we're still safe here?
Of course. The Chief of Police already knew we had killed some protected species, but a small bribe convinced him to lose the warrant for our arrest. You just have to grease the right person's palm in this corrupt country.
But what about Tarzan? He's still after us.
Not for long. The police are going to arrest Tarzan.
Arrest Tarzan? On what grounds?
Disturbing the peace. Tarzan and some guys from Greenpeace went on a hunger strike to save the rain forest.
Are you certain the information is reliable?
Yes! I got it straight from the horse's mouth. The Chief of Police himself.

straight from the horse's mouth
etwas brühwarm erzählt bekommen; etwas aus erster Hand erfahren
(direkt aus dem Maul des Pferdes)

!

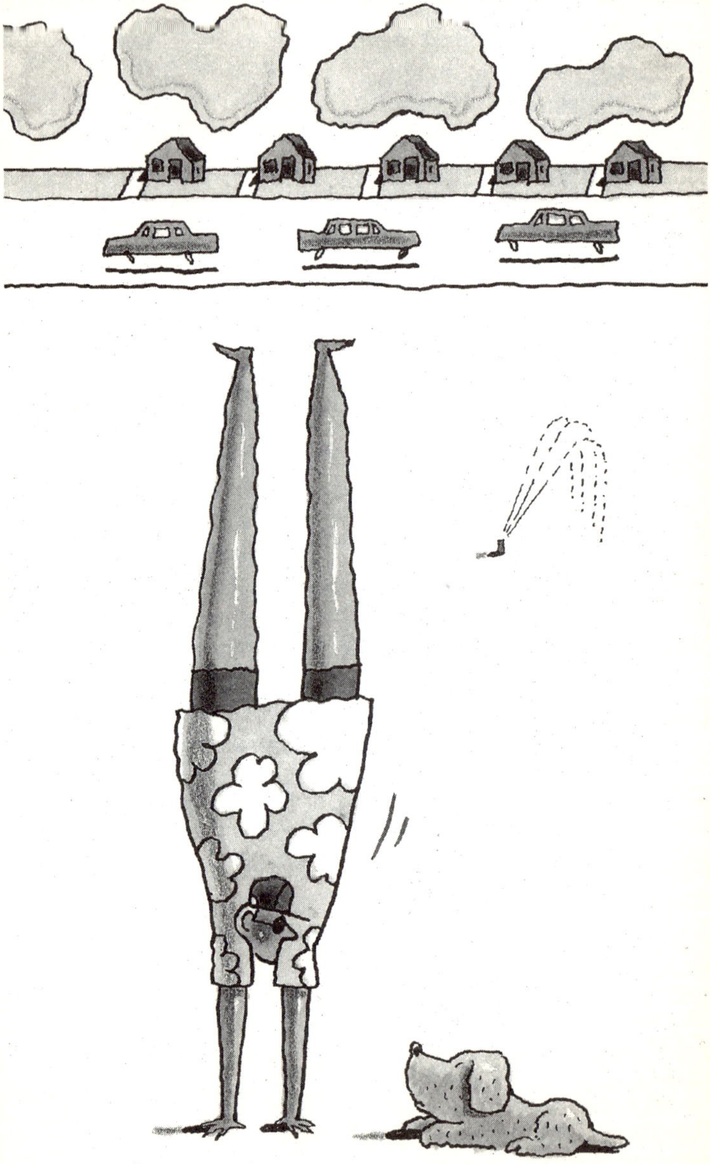

19

Under the stars

Both men looked up at the stars and sat in silence for a moment.
«You know, Priest, there ain't any reason why you couldn't get yourself a woman. You've got plenty of years left in you. My wife's aunt's a widow, you know, maybe you'd like to meet her. She's one heck of a cook.»
«Thanks for offering but no thanks. I've lived alone for the past forty years and I don't think I could learn to share my home with another person, even if it was your pretty wife's aunt. You just can't teach an old dog new tricks.»

20

Out of Africa

Did you hear that Tarzan is out on bail?
Tarzan doesn't concern us anymore. We've stockpiled enough ivory to last us a lifetime. It's time to leave the jungle and give up our life of crime.
But poaching is all I know how to do. Besides, I like hunting animals. I enjoy the thrill of the hunt.
I'm sure we'll find something to keep you busy. We could go to the coast and open a restaurant.
I don't know anything about cooking or running a restaurant.
You'll learn ...
No, you can't teach an old dog new tricks.

You can't teach an old dog new tricks.
Was Hänschen nicht lernt, lernt Hans nimmermehr.
(Einem alten Hund kann man keine neuen Kunststückchen mehr beibringen.)

!

TOPIC 1 VOCABULARY

1 In the Wild West

stamp
Stampfen

howl
Jaulen; Heulen

blazing
lichterloh brennen

to crawl into a warm bed with my Mrs
mit meiner Gattin in ein warmes Bett krabbeln

to spin a yarn
eine Geschichte erzählen

to take one's mind off something/someone
jemanden auf andere Gedanken bringen; von etwas ablenken

2 It's a jungle out there

It's a jungle out there.
Da draußen geht's wüst zu. (Da draußen ist ein Dschungel.)

supposedly
angeblich

loincloth
Lendenschurz

You can say that again.
Da hast du aber Recht; das kannst du zweimal sagen.

natives
Eingeborene

to check someone out
sich jemanden mal genauer anschauen

3 Back East

to wrap
einwickeln

Shoot!
Schieß los! Sag schon!

you was born
typische Slang-«Grammatik»; richtig: you were born

to be like night and day
unterschiedlich wie Tag und Nacht sein

reckless braggart
rücksichtsloser, leichtsinniger Angeber

to fall head over heels in love with someone
siehe «The Human Body» 47/48

to challenge someone to a fight
jemanden zu einem Duell herausfordern

4 Tarzan

Give me a break!
Jetzt mach mal halblang!

to drop out of school
vorzeitig von der Schule abgehen

Taronga Zoo
Zoo in Sydney, Australien

5 Right in the middle of town

glimmer of excitement
ein aufgewühltes Leuchten

to knock the stuffing out of someone
jemanden windelweich hauen

to raise a hand against
die Hand erheben gegen

my own flesh and blood
mein eigen Fleisch und Blut

to cuss and curse
fluchen

to accuse
beschuldigen

fiancée
Verlobte

6 After the rhinoceros hunt

it gives me the jitters
es macht mich nervös

or else
oder es passiert was

to mean business
es wirklich ernst meinen

The bloke is all talk.
Der Typ macht nur Sprüche.

7 Go West, Young Man

to poke
stochern

embers
glühende Asche

pig-headed
stur; starrsinnig

to pick a fight
Streit suchen

It was killing my mother.
Das hat meine Mutter fertig gemacht.

8 By the campfire

He misses us.
Wir fehlen ihm.

to breathe down someone's neck
jemandem im Nacken sitzen

9 An unknown land

bough
dicker Ast

to inch closer to
näher rücken an

The worst is yet to come.
Das dicke Ende (Schlimmste) kommt erst noch.

worries
Sorgen

10 A murder plot

a murder plot
ein Mordkomplott

I've had it.
Jetzt reicht's mir aber.

bloke
Typ

to make someone's life miserable
jemandem das Leben vermiesen

a man after my own heart
ein Mann ganz nach meinem Geschmack

I'm fed up.
Ich hab's satt.

to pump someone full of lead
jemanden mit Blei vollpumpen; umlegen

11 In the wilderness

to shiver
zittern; frösteln

drought
Dürre

crops
Ernte; Erntegut

just barely alive
kaum noch am Leben

12 The new car

a beaut
eine Schönheit

it (had) better be
wehe, wenn nicht

to cry over spilled milk
siehe «Food and Drink» 29/30

baby
hier: das neue Auto

13 In St. Louis

discouraged
entmutigt

to make it to ...
es bis nach ... schaffen

to catch up with someone
jemanden einholen

to relate
berichten

to send for someone
jemanden holen lassen

to be on one's feet again
wieder auf den Beinen sein; alles abgeklärt haben

14 Another accident

to be eaten alive
bei lebendigem Leibe gefressen werden

to wreck
zerstören

15 On the back of a horse

to go into mourning
trauern

dirty scoundrel
elender Schuft

to trick someone
jemanden reinlegen

to steal someone's heart
jemandes Herz stehlen

devastated
am Boden zerstört sein

16 Nerves of steel

We're done for.
Wir sind erledigt.

to pack up and get out of here
zusammenpacken und verschwinden

He likes doing things his own way.
Er erledigt gern alles auf seine Art.

17 At the Ponderosa

to tip back a hat
einen Hut nach oben schieben

buried
begraben

to show up
auftauchen

18 A little money goes a long way

to go a long way
lange vorhalten

protected species
geschützte Arten

bribe
Bestechungsgeld

warrant for an arrest
Haftbefehl

to grease someone's palm
jemanden bestechen

to disturb the peace
öffentliches Ärgernis erregen

reliable
verlässlich

19 Under the stars

ain't
Slang für: am not; aren't; isn't

You've got plenty of years left in you.
Du hast noch viele (gute) Jahre vor dir.

one heck of a ...
ein Wahnsinns...

Thanks for offering but no thanks.
Danke für das Angebot, aber nein danke.

20 Out of Africa

out on bail
gegen Kaution auf freiem Fuß

stockpiled
angehäuft

to last a lifetime
genug für ein ganzes Leben sein

to poach
wildern

TOPIC 1 EXERCISES

1. What's the best answer?

1. Nobody will help you when you really need it if you always
a kill two birds with one stone.
b take the bull by the horns.
c cry wolf.

2. My grandfather refuses to learn how to use a computer because he says
a it's better to let sleeping dogs lie.
b you can't teach an old dog new tricks.
c it kills two birds with one stone.

3. Before I buy this car, I want to
a put it through its paces.
b ruffle its feathers.
c take the bull by the horns.

4. Don't tell her that you broke her glasses. Just
a let sleeping dogs lie.
b put her through her paces.
c take the bull by the horns.

5. I know the story's true, because
a it kills two birds with one stone.
b it's the straw that broke the camel's back.
c I got it straight from the horse's mouth.

6. Don't be afraid of her,
a you can't teach an old dog new tricks.
b her bark is worse than her bite.
c you ruffled her feathers.

2. Say it using an idiom

1. Don't tell your grandmother. You shouldn't say or do things that might make her angry if it isn't really necessary.

2. You sound like you're a very dangerous person, but you really aren't.

3. Don't listen to him, he always warns people of dangers that don't exist.

4. Older people have great difficulty learning how to do new things.

5. I got this information from a very reliable person.

6. I didn't do anything when you said I was rude and stupid, but when you called me a thief, that finally made me angry.

7. When you said he was too fat, you made him angry.

8. Don't worry about possible risks! Just do it!

9. I want to see what this motorcycle can do before I buy it.

10. That will solve two problems with only one effort.

3. Match the phrases

1. I'll never learn to like rap music, I guess you can't…
2. I'm sure they're getting married, because I heard it…
3. The house is n-o-t on fire, you were just…
4. You think I'm a terrible lover? I want a divorce, that's…
5. That exam was difficult, the teacher really…
6. I don't care if it's dangerous. Someone has to…
7. I didn't tell him you failed the exam again, because it's best to…
8. Most people are afraid of Mrs. Gimble, but I know…
9. When you said you didn't like her new dress, you really…
10. I'll take you to the station on my way to work, that way I can…

a. …crying wolf.
b. …put us through our paces.
c. …the straw that broke the camel's back.
d. …kill two birds with one stone.
e. …teach an old dog new tricks.
f. …ruffled her feathers.
g. …her bark is worse than her bite
h. …take the bull by the horns.
i. …straight from the horse's mouth.
j. …let sleeping dogs lie.

Answers: 1. ☐ 2. ☐ 3. ☐ 4. ☐ 5. ☐ 6. ☐ 7. ☐ 8. ☐ 9. ☐ 10. ☐

4. Translate

1. Hab keine Angst. Hunde, die bellen, beißen nicht.

....

....

2. Mach dir keine Sorgen! Der Junge gibt nur falschen Alarm.

....

....

3. Verschwende keine Zeit! Pack's an!

....

....

4. Was Hänschen nicht lernt, lernt Hans nimmermehr.

....

....

5. Auf diese Weise können wir zwei Fliegen mit einer Klappe schlagen.

....

....

6. Bevor wir Herrn Schmidt einstellen, möchte ich ihn auf seine Belastbarkeit prüfen.

....

....

7. Das habe ich aus erster Hand erfahren.

....

....

8. Du hast sie wirklich verärgert.

....

....

9. Schlafende Hunde soll man nicht wecken.

....

....

10. Das ist der Tropfen, der das Fass zum Überlaufen brachte.

....

....

TOPIC 2

FOOD & DRINK

21 On the telephone

Hello, this is George Miller. How may I help you?
Hi, honey. It's me. Do you have time to talk?
Sure. I always have time for you. Have you told everyone the good news?
I didn't have to. They already knew.
What? How did they find out? You haven't gained that much weight.
Well, I made the mistake of trusting my secretary. When I told her, I swore her to secrecy, but that didn't do much good. This morning ten people congratulated me when I stepped into the elevator. She must have spilled the beans right after I told her I was pregnant.

22 Monday morning at work

Jim, you're an idiot!
What's the matter now?
I told you to keep your trap shut no matter what, but this morning when I got to the office, everybody was staring at me as if I had fallen off the moon. It was embarrassing. First I thought I'd forgotten to zip my fly, but then it dawned on me ... You told someone that things got a little out of hand between Joan and me last night, didn't you?
Emm, er, well, I guess I did.
Did you or didn't you?
Yes, I did. But I only told Marion.
Marion? Marion Mann?! She's the biggest blabbermouth in human history. If she knows, the whole company knows. Oh man, I'm in b-i-g trouble. I should've known that you'd spill the beans.

to spill the beans
alles ausplaudern; ein Geheimnis preisgeben
(die Bohnen verschütten)

!

23 The last day at work

What is t-h-a-t?

One of the gifts my colleagues gave me for the baby. It's hideous, isn't it? I think it's supposed to be a giraffe. Everyone was so sweet.

They're all going to miss you. You made a lot of money for them.

Most of them still can't believe it. The firm's most promising young female lawyer quits her job, gives up a six-figure salary and a very bright future to stay at home and be a full-time mother.

Are you sure you're doing the right thing?

Yes. I love my job, but I don't want my child to grow up thinking a stranger is his mother. You can't eat your cake and have it too.

24 The next day, in the office

Well, Jim, thanks to your big mouth everybody seems to know about me and Joan.

You mean, like, everybody, even h-i-m?

No, her husband doesn't suspect a thing. Not yet. But what really bothers me is that Joan doesn't want to get a divorce.

Why not? She obviously likes you more than him.

At first I couldn't figure it out myself, but then things started making sense. The old geezer makes lots of money, they have a great house right on the beach, he buys her all kinds of expensive presents. And for her other needs she has me.

You know what I would tell her?

What?

I'd tell her to choose me or the money. I'd say: «Sorry, babe, but you can't eat your cake and have it too.»

!

to eat one's cake and have it too

man kann nicht alles haben/tun, man muss sich entscheiden (den Kuchen aufessen und ihn trotzdem noch haben)

25 A quiet evening at home

Here's some milk. Want anything else?

Ooh.

What's the matter? Is it time? Should we call the doctor?

No. Relax. Don't worry. The baby was only kicking, letting us know that he's in there.

Can I get you something? Anything, just ask. A pillow or maybe another magazine, or maybe I should ...

Slow down. I'm fine. Being pregnant is not a disease, you know.

Sorry, I guess I'm already overdoing it a little. I just want you to be all right. I hope I'm not getting on your nerves. Maybe you're regretting the day we got married.

Not at all. The day we got married was the happiest day in my life, because I got the cream of the crop. Nobody could be a better husband.

26 A step up the ladder

Jim, you won't believe what just happened ...

What?

I just got a phone call from Joan's husband, Mr. Morris.

Uh-oh! He found out, didn't he?

No, he didn't. Worse!

What could be worse than that?

He asked me to join his company, Morris Enterprises. Joan gave him my name.

I can't believe she did that.

Me neither! But he actually wants to pay me a fortune. He said it was an easy decision to make. Of all the candidates he reviewed I was definitely the cream of the crop.

the cream of the crop
der/das Allerbeste; allererste Sahne
(der Rahm der Ernte)

!

27

The first day at home

Are you sure you'll be all right?

Yes, George. Don't worry. Now get going or you'll be late for work.

Are there enough disposable diapers left?

Yes, George. I just opened a new box.

And don't forget to put some of that powder on her bottom when you're changing the diaper.

We've gone over everything a million times. I've read all the books, and the nurse at the hospital gave me some pointers. Don't worry.

Oh, and don't forget that the plumber is coming by to check the swimming pool.

George, that's enough. I can handle everything. I'm sure we won't have any problems. It'll be a piece of cake.

28

28 The new job

Well Jim, do you think I should accept the offer and work for Morris?

And fool around with his wife at the same time? No way! You must be out of your mind to even consider it.

But Jim, I'll be making twice as much at Morris Enterprises.

You seriously think you can work there a-n-d stay out of trouble? What if somebody finds out about you and the boss's wife?

No problem! Nobody's going to find out. It'll be a piece of cake!

!

a piece of cake
das ist ein Kinderspiel; kinderleicht
(ein Stück Kuchen)

29 The evening of the first day

Hi, honey, I'm home. — Oh my God, what happened in here? Is the baby okay?

Yes, she's fine — now. She went to sleep half an hour ago. Oh, George, she cried all day. I changed her and I fed her and I rocked her, but she wouldn't stop. When she finally settled down, I decided to do some painting. I was carrying the paint out to the garage, when I tripped and dropped it onto the carpet.

It's all right. It could have happened to anybody.

But the carpet is ruined. It took us ages to find one just the right color. We'll never get it clean.

Hey, stop that. We'll just have to buy another one. It's no use crying over spilled milk.

30 A telephone conversation

Hi, Jim. This is Owen. How's life in your part of the world?

Owen?! Where are you calling from?

I'm in Vancouver on a business trip. Guess who came along.

Joan, of course. I already know.

How did you find out? We didn't tell anyone.

Well, my new girlfriend is pretty friendly with Mr. Morris' personal secretary, the woman that knows everything. When Joan told Mr. Morris something about visiting her sick grandmother, he got suspicious. He hired a private eye and had her followed. It didn't take the secretary long to find out. And once she knew ...

Shit! What are we going to do now? There goes my job.

Oh well, too late now. No use crying over spilled milk.

! **to cry over spilled milk**

Was passiert ist, ist passiert.

Geschehenes lässt sich nicht ungeschehen machen.

(wegen verschütteter Milch weinen)

31 TV time

Ha, ha, ha. This movie is hilarious, don't you think? Honey? Honey? Wake up!

Wha-what? Oh, I'm sorry, George. I'm so tired I can't keep my eyes open anymore. I think I'll turn in.

But you wanted to watch this movie. I turned off the basketball game, so we could watch it.

Yes, I know. I really wanted to watch it, but it's no use. I've been on my feet all day, running around, taking care of the baby. I didn't think it was going to be so exhausting. I hardly have time to sit down and drink a cup of coffee.

Do I detect a note of regret?

No, well, it's just, sometimes I wonder if I can really handle it. I'm afraid I've bitten off more than I can chew.

32 Starting over

In a way I'm glad it's all over now. That thing with Joan was a lot of stress. It's all for the best that she went back to her husband. And then there was the new job. You were right, Jim, it wasn't easy keeping my private life out of the office. I was constantly on edge. A typical case of biting off more of than you can chew.

to bite off more than one can chew
mehr in Angriff nehmen, als man bewältigen kann;
sich zu viel zumuten
(mehr abbeißen, als man kauen kann)

!

33 George's afternoon with the baby

Hello, dear. Did you have a good time?
Yes, I did. I-I can't believe my eyes. This place looks fantastic. George, how did you do it?
Well, it wasn't too difficult. I always was pretty good with a mop and a vacuum cleaner.
I'm impressed. Did the baby give you much trouble?
None at all. She slept through the whole afternoon.
Something smells good. What is it?
Well, I finished cleaning early, so I baked some cookies. Want some?
Unbelievable! I told everyone I was doing a good job around the house, but I guess I have to eat my words. George, you're a better housewife than I ever could be.

34 Owen drops a bombshell

Hi, Jim, have you heard the latest?
No, what is it this time?
Joan is pregnant.
Really? Who's the father, you or Mr. Morris?
According to Joan, it's me.
Nice twist of fate. First Morris finds out that his wife has an affair, and then, to add insult to injury, her lover gets her pregnant.
Joan is getting a divorce.
But you told me it was over.
Not any more. I can't desert our love child! It was better to eat my words and take her back.

!

to eat one's words
zurücknehmen, was man gesagt hat
(seine Wörter essen)

35 The discussion

Well, how is it? Do you like the chicken?
George, this is absolutely delicious.
Oh, come on. You're just saying that.
No, I really mean it. I had forgotten how well you can cook. You really put me to shame. Maybe you should stay at home, and I'll go back to work.
Well, that might not be such a bad idea. You know I haven't been happy with the way my boss has been treating me lately. Maybe I should just quit for a while and make myself useful here around the house.
Are you serious?
Yes, I am. I'm sure your firm would take you back in an instant. Don't be old-fashioned. It doesn't really matter which one of us brings home the bacon.

36 Getting married

Hi, Jim.
Hi there. How's life? Have you found a job yet?
No, unfortunately not. But I d-o have some news for you: Joan and I are getting married.
It's about time.
Yeah, I know. She's six months pregnant and it's beginning to show. But now I'm getting cold feet. I just can't see myself as the responsible family man. No more fooling around, no more rich women to take care of the bills. No more sports cars, no more tailored suits, no more dream vacations. Do I strike you as the kind of guy who could take care of a family and bring home the bacon?

to bring home the bacon
die Brötchen nach Hause bringen; den Lebensunterhalt verdienen
(den Schinkenspeck nach Hause bringen)

!

37 Tho docision

Well, hello. Tell me, how was your first day back in the rat race?

Terrific. It's really great to be back as a part of the team. In fact, I didn't really realize how much I missed it until I walked into my old office and took my first call. It was an irate client upset about something, so I had to smooth his ruffled feathers. I loved it. I'm better at doing business than housework. Being a housewife was definitely not my cup of tea.

38 Married life

Well Jim, what about you and your girlfriend? When are you going to be a married man like me?

Us? We've never even talked about it once. You know, we believe in open relationships. No obligations, no pressure. It's all very relaxed and laid-back.

Good for you.

How are things between you and Joan?

Not so good. Sometimes I really wish I was single again. Every night the kid is screaming at the top of her lungs. It's a nightmare. I never get enough sleep. I'm really not enjoying this. Being a father is just not my cup of tea.

!

to be one's cup of tea
jemandem liegen; nach jemandes Geschmack sein (jemandes Tasse Tee sein)

39 The result

Here you are. A nice, cool glass of white wine. Would you like some strawberries?

George, what's going on here? First, you arrange for your mother to take care of the baby. And then you make me my favorite meal. Now you're serving me wine and strawberries. I think you want something from me. What? A new vacuum cleaner?

You see through me so easily. Well, I was thinking it might be nice to have another baby to take care of.

Another baby? Are you nuts? Having a baby was the most painful experience I've ever had, and I'm not ready for that again. Sorry, but you can't butter me up with wine and strawberries. N-O, no way.

40 All's well that ends well

Man, I'm the happiest man in the world.

You're always good for a surprise. A month ago you hated your life, your wife, your kid. What's happened this time?

We split up. It was the best move for all of us.

And Joan. What happened to Joan?

She's back with her ex. It's all for the best. See, Morris is rich. When I brought home the bacon, it was always hard to make ends meet. Now my worries are over. All I need is a better job. I'm sick of frying burgers at McDonald's.

Well, why don't you call up Mr. Yakamoto and invite him to lunch at his favorite restaurant. If you butter him up, he might give you back your old job.

to butter someone up
jemandem Honig ums Maul schmieren; jemanden umgarnen; sich bei jemandem anbiedern (jemanden einbuttern)

!

21 On the telephone

to gain weight
zunehmen; dicker werden

to swear someone to secrecy
jemanden zur Geheimhaltung verpflichten

not to do much good
nicht viel nützen

pregnant
schwanger

22 Monday morning at work

to keep one's trap shut
den Mund halten

as if I had fallen off the moon
als wäre ich vom Mond gefallen

embarrassing
peinlich

to zip one's fly
den Hosenlatz schließen

to dawn on someone
etwas dämmert einem; jemandem geht ein Licht auf

something got a little out of hand
die Sache lief ein wenig aus dem Ruder

blabbermouth
Tratschmaul

23 The last day at work

hideous
abgrundtief hässlich

it's supposed to be a ...
soll ein ... sein

six-figure salary
sechsstelliges Gehalt

24 The next day, in the office

to figure something out
etwas verstehen

old geezer
alter Knacker

25 A quiet evening at home

to get on someone's nerves
jemandem auf die Nerven gehen

26 A step up the ladder

Uh-oh!
Ausruf der Überraschung, verbunden mit der Ahnung kommenden Unheils

fortune
ein Haufen Geld; Vermögen

to review
überprüfen; evaluieren

27 The first day at home

disposable diapers
Papierwindeln; britisches Englisch: nappy

bottom
Popo; Hintern

to go over something
etwas durchsprechen

to give some pointers
ein paar Tipps geben

I can handle it.
Ich schaffe das schon.

28 The new job

to fool around with
rummachen mit

No way!
Niemals!

to be out of one's mind
übergeschnappt sein

to make twice as much
doppelt so viel verdienen

29 The evening of the first day

to rock
wiegen

to settle down
sich beruhigen

to take ages
eine Ewigkeit dauern

It's no use.
Es ist zwecklos.

30 A telephone conversation

to guess who
mal raten, wer

to be pretty friendly with someone
mit jemandem auf gutem Fuß stehen

to get suspicious
Verdacht schöpfen

private eye
Privatdetektiv

There goes my ...!
Mein ... ist futsch!

31 TV time

hilarious
sehr komisch

to turn in
ins Bett gehen

Do I detect a note of regret?
Höre ich da irgendwie ein leichtes Bedauern raus?

to wonder if
sich fragen, ob

to handle
bewerkstelligen

32 Starting over

to be all for the best
wirklich gar nicht so schlimm sein

to be on edge
angespannt sein

33 George's afternoon with the baby

I can't believe my eyes.
Ich traue meinen Augen nicht.

to give someone trouble
jemandem Schwierigkeiten machen

34 Owen drops a bombshell

to drop a bombshell
eine Nachricht, die wie eine Bombe einschlägt, verkünden

twist of fate
Zufall; Ironie des Schicksals

to add insult to injury
Wer den Schaden hat, braucht für den Spott nicht zu sorgen. (zur Verletzung auch noch die Beleidigung hinzufügen)

divorce
Scheidung

to desert someone
jemanden sitzen lassen

35 The discussion

to put someone to shame
jemanden in den Schatten stellen

in an instant
sofort

36 Getting married

to get cold feet
kalte Füße bekommen

to strike someone as
auf jemanden den Eindruck machen als

37 The decision

rat race
Karrieredruck (Rattenrennen)

irate
wütend; zornig

to smooth
besänftigen

ruffled feathers
siehe «Animal Kingdom» 3/4

38 Married life

laid-back
locker

Good for you.
Schön für dich.

at the top of one's lungs
aus vollem Halse (schreien)

39 The result

to see through someone
jemanden durchschauen

to be nuts
verrückt sein

40 All's well that ends well

All's well that ends well.
Ende gut, alles gut.

to be good for a surprise
für eine Überraschung gut sein

to split up
sich trennen

ex
Ex-Ehepartner

to bring home the bacon
siehe «Food and Drink» 35/36

to make ends meet
siehe «Odds and Ends» 61/62

1. What's the best answer?

1. She said that I'm a loser, but some day I'll prove she is wrong and she'll
- **a** spill the beans.
- **b** cry over spilled milk.
- **c** eat her words.

2. Don't worry. I'll have no problems fixing this,
- **a** it's a piece of cake.
- **b** it's not my cup of tea.
- **c** it's the cream of the crop.

3. I'm so glad we decided to hire him,
- **a** he's a piece of cake.
- **b** he's not my cup of tea.
- **c** he's the cream of the crop.

4. Remember, if you buy those new shoes, you won't have any money left for a ticket to the movies tonight,
- **a** you shouldn't bite off more than you can chew.
- **b** you can't bring home the bacon.
- **c** you can't eat your cake and have it too.

5. I don't like playing chess,
- **a** it's not my cup of tea.
- **b** it's no use crying over spilled milk.
- **c** I can't eat my cake and have it too.

6. Now that my husband is unemployed I have to
- **a** butter him up.
- **b** bring home the bacon.
- **c** spill the beans.

2. Say it using an idiom

1. You know that I was fired!? Who told you my secret?

2. If you say and do nice things to him, he might let you drive his new car.

3. You can't do both things. You must choose one.

4. Babysitting is something he really enjoys and he's very good at it.

5. This teacher is the best teacher in our entire school.

6. Now that I don't live with my parents anymore, I have to earn my own money.

7. Learning English is very easy.

8. I will make you admit you said something that wasn't true.

9. Don't complain about things that have already happened and can't be changed.

10. He tried to do more than he was capable of doing.

3. Match the phrases

1. You'll never be able to fix that. Just tell him…
2. Your toy is broken and we can't repair it, so…
3. Paul is an excellent cook. I'd say…
4. No, Barbara never said a word,…
5. He can do it easily. He said…
6. He has to make a decision, either he goes to Spain or saves money for a new car. I told him…
7. My parents are very modern. My father stays at home and my mother…
8. Daniel really hates sports. Basketball…
9. He only said that I am beautiful, because…
10. Lisa said Clinton would never be elected President, but in the end…

- **a.** …you shouldn't cry over spilled milk.
- **b.** …he can't eat his cake and have it too.
- **c.** …she had to eat her words.
- **d.** …he is the cream of the crop.
- **e.** …brings home the bacon.
- **f.** …is not his cup of tea.
- **g.** …you bit off more than you can chew.
- **h.** …it was a piece of a cake.
- **i.** …he wants to butter me up.
- **j.** …she didn't spill the beans.

Answers: 1. ☐ 2. ☐ 3. ☐ 4. ☐ 5. ☐ 6. ☐ 7. ☐ 8. ☐ 9. ☐ 10. ☐

4. Translate

1. Geschehenes lässt sich nicht ungeschehen machen.

....

....

2. Wer hat alles ausgeplaudert?

....

....

3. Er musste zurücknehmen, was er gesagt hatte.

....

....

4. Das ist ein Kinderspiel.

....

....

5. Das liegt mir nicht.

....

....

6. Du kannst nicht alles haben, du musst dich entscheiden.

....

....

7. Wie können wir ihn weich kriegen?

....

....

8. Ich glaube, ich habe mir mehr aufgehalst, als ich schaffen kann.

....

....

9. Dieser Mann ist der allerbeste.

....

....

10. Wer verdient den Lebensunterhalt in deiner Familie?

....

....

TOPIC 3

THE HUMAN BODY

41 A home in the suburbs

Mary Jones has a terrible headache. The television is blaring and her children are screaming.
«Be quiet, you kids! Your dad is trying to sleep and if you wake him up, he'll hit the ceiling!»
The children's squeals continue and suddenly the dog joins in, howling and barking. Mary closes her eyes and groans.
«That's it, the straw that broke the camel's back. Shut up this instant and turn off that TV. If I hear a peep out of anybody, you'll be sorry.»
Silence settles over the house. Mary turns and walks to the bathroom. As she turns the doorknob, the TV is switched on again and the children start screaming.
«They never listen. Those kids are a pain in the ass.»

42 Peggy goes shopping

Al, I'm going shopping. Do you need anything?
Yes, Peg, I could use a six-pack and about three bags of potato chips.
Oh, Al, with your gut? You've got the biggest beer belly in the whole neighborhood. Besides, if I don't waste money on beer and chips, I'll have more to spend on things we really need.
Like new clothes for the kids?
No, new lipstick for me. Avon has a new shade of red for only $29.95. — Oh, by the way, I'm a little short on cash. Where's the credit card?
Oh Peg, just take my wallet and leave me alone. I work hard, and I'd like a little peace and quiet. When it comes to shopping and money, you're a real pain in the neck.

a pain in the ass/neck
eine Nervensäge
(ein Schmerz im Arsch/Nacken) !

43

In the bathroom mirror

Mary slowly undresses and turns on the tap in the bathtub. Steam begins to condense on the edges of the mirror over the sink, but she can clearly see the wrinkles under her eyes and the grey hairs above her ears in the middle of the glass.

«And they once said I was a real beauty,» she reminisces about the days before screaming kids and barking dogs. Of course, that hadn't meant much back then, coming from the wrong side of the tracks. Her father, a filthy drunk, had gone out one night, never to return. With no other skills, her mother had turned to prostitution to keep food in their mouths. Everyone at Mary's school, the pupils and the teachers, knew about her mother. No one was her friend. They all looked down their noses at her.

44

The latest gossip

Al, did you hear what Marcie had to say the other day?

No, Peg, I didn't and I don't want to hear it now. I want to watch TV.

But Al, you have to hear this.

All right then, what did she say?

Well, it might hurt your feelings...

Then keep it to yourself. I'm not interested in Marcie's gossip anyway.

But I've just got to tell someone. She said you're a good-for-nothing bum, and you're wasting your life as a shoe salesman.

She said that? Some friend she is, looking down her nose at a hard-working, tax-paying man like me.

!

to look down one's nose at
jemanden/etwas verachten; auf jemanden herabschauen (die Nase entlang nach unten blicken)

45 In New York

Mary slips into the soothing hot water, and the heat begins to loosen the knots in her neck. She thinks back to another bathtub in a small apartment on 42nd Street in New York. She had often dozed in that tub after work, building castles in the air, dreaming of a handsome husband and a mink coat and a maid.
Shortly after she had graduated, she packed her suitcase, kissed her careworn mother good-bye and moved to New York where she found a job as a secretary at the United Nations. That was the most exciting time in her life. She had met important foreign dignitaries and politicians, and once she even rubbed elbows with the President.

46 An invitation

But Al, it would be so exciting. Just imagine, you and me and the mayor.
Sorry Peg, but I'm against it. The jerk is just like the rest of them, promising «No new taxes» before the election, but as soon as they make themselves comfortable in that big leather chair in City Hall, they raise taxes anyway. I'm not going to any banquet to support that mayor. It's against my principles to rub shoulders with a bum like that.

to rub elbows/shoulders
am gleichen Ort sein; in Kontakt kommen
(Ellbogen/Schultern reiben)

!

47

At a party in Greenwich Village

For the first time in her life, people treated Mary as an equal. She seldom spent an evening alone. Her roommate Paula, a fashion model whose face was often on the cover of «Vogue», rubbed shoulders with lots of artists and musicians, and the parties she went to were always wild.

It was at one of those parties in Greenwich Village that she met Don. Weaving through the room in a drunken stupor, he poured his drink down the front of Mary's dress. When she looked into his big brown eyes, she didn't get angry; her heart stood still. She wanted to marry this man and no other. She was head over heels in love.

48

Family life

Al, I'm a little concerned about Kelly.

Kelly? Kelly who?

Oh, Al! Kelly, our daughter.

Oh, her. Well, she isn't getting any more money out of me. You've already confiscated my wallet.

No, be serious. Lately she's been bringing home this guy with long, greasy hair, a ring in his nose, a tattoo on his left buttock ...

How on earth do you know what's on his left buttock?

Well, I took a peek while he was taking a shower.

I knew I should've fixed that shower curtain.

I think Kelly and that guy are really getting serious. They're always together.

Good. If he's head over heels in love with her, maybe he'll start paying her bills.

!

head over heels in love
bis über beide Ohren verliebt
(Kopf über Ferse verliebt)

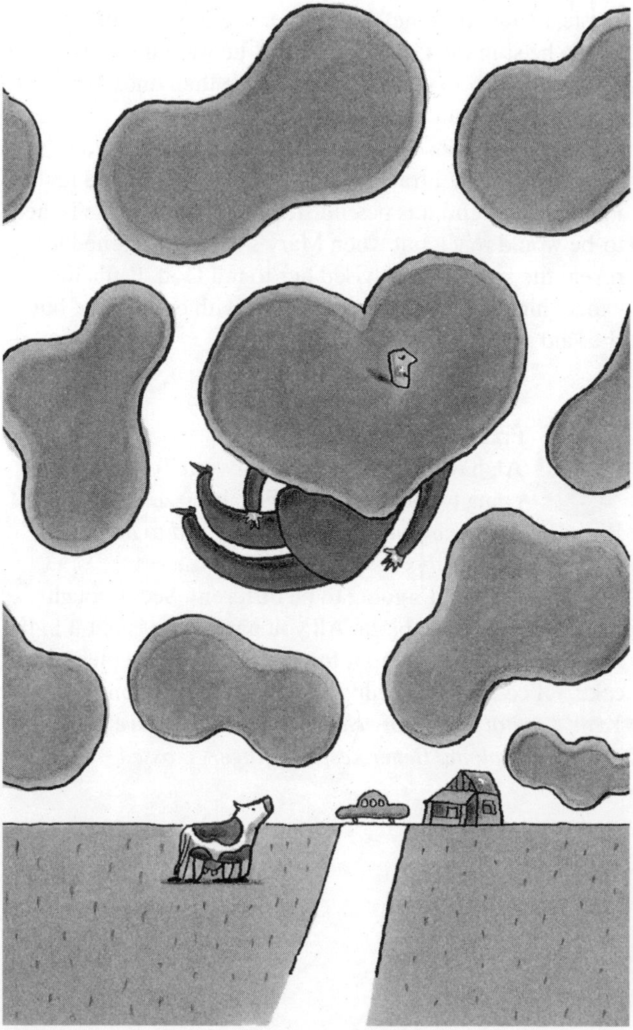

49

In the back seat of his car

Instead of following in his father's footsteps, Don, the black sheep of the family, had tried his luck at music, living off money his mother secretly sent him. When he stumbled into Mary's life, he was an unsuccessful alcoholic, even suicidal at times. More than once Mary took a loaded gun out of his hand.
It was in the back seat of his car that their first child was conceived. Mary, afraid of Don's reaction, confided first in Paula. Her friend was pessimistic about the way the father-to-be would react, but when Mary's body threatened to reveal the secret, she advised her to tell Don. Paula didn't expect him to welcome Mary's baby with open arms, but she said she'd keep her fingers crossed.

50

Pizza chez Peg

Al, have I got a surprise for you! Tonight I'm going to make you a delicious pizza.
Well, Peg, last time you tried to cook we had to buy a new kitchen ... Maybe this isn't such a good idea.
No, Al, this time it's going to be different. See, I bought this new microwave pizza. All you have to do is put it in the microwave oven and zap it for 10 minutes. It's a piece of cake. Of course, something could always go wrong ...
Yeah, I'm not taking any chances. The microwave'll probably explode. Better keep my fingers crossed.

!

to keep one's fingers crossed
jemandem die Daumen drücken
(die Finger gekreuzt halten)

51 In a bar

She knew where to find him. Don spent most of his time in a seedy bar on Broadway, a dark hole that smelled of cigarettes, cheap whiskey and vomit, and it was there that Mary broke the news to him.
He looked at her with those big brown eyes, bloodshot and tinged with yellow, and started laughing. He was sure his excessive drinking had made him infertile and that he could never father a child. He simply didn't believe her. He thought she was pulling his leg.

52 On the telephone

Well, Al, today you're really going to be surprised when you get home.
Oh great! Did you wreck the car?
No, Al, I've got a nice surprise for you: I cleaned the house and washed and ironed your clothes — even your underwear. And I've just started preparing a three-course gourmet meal for you.
Did you really?
Of course not. I was only pulling your leg. Nobody in their right mind would ever touch y-o-u-r dirty underwear!

to pull someone's leg
jemandem einen Bären aufbinden; jemanden veräppeln (jemandes Bein ziehen)

53 At city hall

When Don finally sobered up and Mary mentioned marriage, he disappeared, off on another drinking binge.
As the weeks flew by and Don didn't reappear, Mary turned in desperation to his mother for help. The old woman missed her son and hoped that a baby would make him settle down. Tracking him down was easy enough, persuading him to marry was not. Don only laughed at his mother, but she had one last trick up her sleeve. She withheld the very money that kept him out of the gutter, and ten days later Don knuckled under. He and Mary got married at city hall.

54 A piece of advice

I'm telling you, son, that's the first thing you have to learn when you get married.
You mean I'll have to learn to be a loving and caring husband?
No, you have to learn to knuckle under.

!

to knuckle under
nachgeben; sich einer stärkeren Macht unterwerfen
(sich den Fingerknöcheln unterwerfen)

55

The house is still

When Don Jr. was born, Don was working in an nondescript office and started hitting the bottle after hours. His problem gradually worsened as three more babies joined their family.
With a sigh, Mary steps out of the tub, stops and listens. Quiet. No screaming, no crying, no barking. Then gunshots pierce the silence, one, two, three, four, five.
She stumbles into the living room. The sight that greets her turns her stomach, forcing her to bend over and vomit.

56

Barf!

I think the human race would be better off without men — including you, Al.
But Peg, men have ways to make women happy — if you know what I mean.
You call that happiness? With you it lasts for about thirty seconds and then it's over. No, the disadvantages by far outweigh the advantages. Besides, just looking at you in the morning is enough to turn my stomach.

to turn one's stomach
den Magen umdrehen; jemandem Übelkeit verursachen (jemandes Magen umdrehen)

!

57 In the living room

Her four children lie on the living room floor, their lifeless bodies relaxed as if they were asleep. Slowly, blood drips off their fingers, their elbows, the tips of their noses, and seeps into the carpet. The smallest still holds onto the dead dog.
A noise in the bedroom causes her to flinch. She turns in that direction.
«Come on, Mary, he's your husband. Be brave. What did your mother always say? Don't panic. Keep a stiff upper lip.»

58 A disaster

Oh Peg, I don't know how much longer I can take this. It's too much. The mental stress, the anxiety, the agony of waiting. If this goes on for just one more hour, I'll have a nervous breakdown.
Keep a stiff upper lip. I'm sure they'll have the TV fixed before tonight's ball game.

!

to keep a stiff upper lip
die Ohren steifhalten; sich nicht entmutigen lassen
(eine steife Oberlippe behalten)

59 In the bedroom

«Don, are you in here?» Then she sees him sitting on the bed, a gun in his hand.
«They wouldn't shut up,» he mumbles, «so I made them.»
«You monster!» Mary slaps a hand over her mouth, but it's too late. The words already hang in the air.
Don looks away, places the gun on his temple, his finger on the trigger. «Yes, dear, you're right. You took the words right out of my mouth.»

60 Who's afraid of mowing the lawn?

Al, it's time we did something about the lawn. It looks terrible out there. Maybe you could mow the grass.
Me? Do you actually think that I would want to waste my weekend cutting grass? I can think of better things to do with my time, like watching TV and drinking beer.
I can't do it either. I might break a fingernail or mess my hair up. Well, if you're not interested, how about making the kids work for their keep?
I was just going to suggest that myself. You took the words right out of my mouth.

!

to take the words right out of one's mouth
jemandem das Wort aus dem Munde nehmen
(jemandem die Wörter direkt aus seinem Mund nehmen)

41 A home in the suburbs

to blare
dröhnen

to hit the ceiling
(vor Wut) in die Luft gehen

squeal
Gequieke

to bark
bellen

to groan
tief seufzen

the straw that broke the camel's back
siehe «Animal Kingdom» 13/14

doorknob
In den USA gibt's keine Türklinken, sondern Drehgriffe: Türknauf

42 Peggy goes shopping

six-pack
Bierdosen-Sechserpackung

gut
Bauch

beer belly
Bierbauch

neighborhood
Stadtviertel

to be a little short on cash
ein bisschen knapp bei Kasse sein

I'd like a little peace and quiet.
Ich möchte meine Ruhe haben.

when it comes to ...
was ... angeht/betrifft

43 In the bathroom mirror

to reminisce
in Erinnerungen schwelgen

the wrong side of the tracks
aus ärmlichen Verhältnissen (die falsche Seite der Schienen)

a filthy drunk
ein widerlicher Alkoholiker

44 The latest gossip

keep it to yourself
behalt's für dich

gossip
Tratsch und Klatsch

a good-for-nothing bum
ein Kerl, der zu nichts zu gebrauchen ist

Some friend she is!
Das ist mir ja 'ne schöne Freundin!

45 In New York

to doze
dösen; schlummern

to build castles in the air
Luftschlösser bauen

mink coat
Nerzmantel

careworn
von Sorgen gezeichnet

dignitary
Würdenträger

46 An invitation

mayor
Bürgermeister

jerk
Depp; Schwachkopf

It's against my principles.
Das ist gegen meine Prinzipien.

47 At a party in Greenwich Village

to treat someone as an equal
jemanden wie seinesgleichen behandeln

to rub shoulders with someone
siehe «The Human Body» 45/46

in a drunken stupor
in einem Zustand völligen Betrunkenseins

Her heart stood still.
Ihr stand das Herz still.

48 Family life

to be concerned about
sich Sorgen machen um

greasy
fettig

buttock
Hinterbacke

to take a peek
einen Blick werfen

They are getting serious.
Sie kriegen langsam eine feste Beziehung.

49 In the back seat of his car

to follow in someone's footsteps
in jemandes Fußstapfen treten

the black sheep of the family
das schwarze Schaf der Familie

to try one's luck at ...
sich an ... versuchen

to live off money (that)
von Geld leben, das

to conceive
schwanger werden

to welcome someone with open arms
jemanden mit offenen Armen willkommen heißen

50 Pizza chez Peg

to zap
in der Mikrowelle aufwärmen

a piece of cake
siehe «Food and Drink» 27/28

to take a chance
etwas riskieren

better
kurz für: I had better = Es empfiehlt sich, ...

51 In a bar

seedy
runtergekommen

vomit
Erbrochenes

to break the news
eine (meist traurige) Nachricht mitteilen

bloodshot eyes
gerötete Augen

infertile
unfruchtbar

to father a child
ein Kind zeugen

52 On the telephone

to iron
bügeln

three-course gourmet meal
Feinschmeckermenü in drei Gängen

in one's right mind
bei klarem Verstand; im Vollbesitz seiner geistigen Kräfte

53 At city hall

to sober up
ausnüchtern

drinking binge
Saufgelage

to track someone down
jemanden aufspüren

to have something up one's sleeve
siehe «Odds and Ends» 141/142

to withhold
zurückhalten

the very money that
genau das Geld, das

gutter
Gosse

54 A piece of advice

loving and caring
liebend und treu sorgend

55 The house is still

nondescript
sich durch nichts auszeichnend; stinknormal

to hit the bottle
saufen

after hours
nach Geschäftsschluss

to vomit
sich übergeben

by far
bei weitem

56 Barf!

Barf!
Kotz!

to have ways
Mittel und Wege haben

The disadvantages outweigh the advantages.
Die Nachteile überwiegen die Vorteile.

57 In the living room

to seep into
versickern in

to flinch
zusammenzucken

58 A disaster

nervous breakdown
Nervenzusammenbruch

ball game
Baseballspiel

59 In the bedroom

to mumble
nuscheln

temple
Schläfe

trigger
Abzug einer Pistole

60 Who's afraid of mowing the lawn?

lawn
Rasen

to work for one's keep
für Kost und Logis arbeiten

TOPIC 3 EXERCISES

1. What's the best answer?

1. I never want to babysit that kid again. She's
- **a** head over heels in love.
- **b** a pain in the neck.
- **c** pulling my leg.

2. In times of trouble, don't worry. You should
- **a** knuckle under.
- **b** look down your nose at others.
- **c** keep a stiff upper lip.

3. Just because she's rich and I'm poor, she thinks she can
- **a** take the words right out of my mouth.
- **b** look down her nose at me.
- **c** rub shoulders with me.

4. It smelled so bad, it
- **a** turned my stomach.
- **b** pulled my leg.
- **c** was a pain in the neck.

5. If we put enough pressure on him, eventually he'll
- **a** keep a stiff upper lip.
- **b** knuckle under.
- **c** be head over heels.

6. Ha, ha! No! I'm not really pregnant. I was just
- **a** rubbing elbows with you.
- **b** looking down my nose at you.
- **c** pulling your leg.

2. Say it using an idiom

1. You said exactly what I wanted to say.

2. Stop crying! Be brave!

3. The sight of blood makes me feel ill.

4. I'll never do what they are trying to force me to do.

5. I'm only kidding you!

6. I hope I'll win the race. Wish me luck!

7. I love her very much.

8. When I lived in Hollywood, I often met famous actors at parties.

9. My little sister always annoys me.

10. He thinks I am inferior, because I didn't study at Harvard.

3. Match the phrases

1. He's so handsome. When she meets him,…
2. I completely agree with you,…
3. She couldn't say no to them any longer,…
4. Joan didn't cry when she got the injection,…
5. The film was so violent and bloody, that…
6. No, she doesn't really know Woody Allen,…
7. Susan wants a divorce, because…
8. Even though she thought he wouldn't get the new job,…
9. Steve doesn't come from a very good family. I'm afraid…
10. There's no spider in your hair. When she told you that,…

a. …she had to knuckle under.
b. …it turned her stomach.
c. …she still kept her fingers crossed.
d. …she kept a stiff upper lip.
e. …she'll look down her nose at him.
f. …she'll fall head over heels in love with him.
g. …her husband is a pain in the ass.
h. …she was only pulling your leg.
i. …she's never rubbed shoulders with anybody famous.
j. …you took the words right out of my mouth.

Answers: 1. ☐ 2. ☐ 3. ☐ 4. ☐ 5. ☐ 6. ☐ 7. ☐ 8. ☐ 9. ☐ 10. ☐

4. Translate

1. Rohes Fleisch verursacht mir Übelkeit.

....

....

2. Halt die Ohren steif!

....

....

3. Du hast mir das Wort aus dem Munde genommen.

....

....

4. Er wird schließlich nachgeben.

....

....

5. Meine Frau ist eine echte Nervensäge.

....

....

6. In London bin ich in Kontakt mit sehr wichtigen Personen gekommen.

....

....

7. Du solltest nicht auf ihn herabschauen.

....

....

8. Sie ist bis über beide Ohren in ihn verliebt.

....

....

9. Veräppelst du mich?

....

....

10. Drück mir die Daumen.

....

....

TOPIC

4

MONEY & BUSINESS

61 A new house pet

Oh, Jane, he's so cute! What a sweet little dog!
Sweet? That's what I thought when Tom first brought him home, but that dog is a monster. He barks all the time, he pees on the furniture, and he's eating us out of house and home.
Oh, I don't believe it. This little dog ...
Well, I'll let you be the judge. Take him home and ...
Oh, I wish I could, but dogs cost money and we don't have any. Ever since my husband lost his job, we're having a hard time making ends meet.

62 Home after work

Bills, bills, bills, that's the only mail we ever get. I'm sick and tired of it.
But now we have a beautiful house, new furniture and a brand-new car. And if we work hard, we'll be out of the red in about forty years.
Forty years? We'll both be sixty-four! We're wasting the best years of our lives paying off the house and the car. We're working our fingers to the bone, but at the end of the month we still can't make ends meet.

to make ends meet
finanziell über die Runden kommen
(Enden zusammenführen)

!

63 A nosy neighbor

What's wrong, Jane? Did the dog make a mess again?

No. It's Mrs. O'Reilly, our next-door neighbor. Tom and I had an argument about the dog last night, and we forgot the window was open. This morning all the women in the neighborhood called me up to give me the number of their divorce lawyer. Mrs. O'Reilly must have been listening to us again, and she didn't waste any time spreading gossip. She's more concerned about what her neighbors are doing than about what's happening in her own house. It's horrible.
I wish she'd learn to mind her own business.

64 A concerned friend

Fred asked me today what's the matter with us. He wanted to know why we stay home all the time and don't go out anymore ...

Well, if he had to pay off our mortgage, he'd stay home too. Just going to the movies sets us back $ 30. Next time he makes any remarks, tell him to mind his own business.

! **to mind one's own business**
sich um seine eigenen Angelegenheiten kümmern
(sich um sein eigenes Geschäft kümmern)

65 Four eggs and a loaf of bread

Hi, Jane. I brought over the stuff you called me about. Four eggs and a loaf of bread.

Oh Anne, this is so embarrassing, but there's nothing in the refrigerator, and I don't have a red cent left. That dog is costing us a fortune. Dog food is so expensive, not to mention the bills for Dr. Harriot ...

Dr. Harriot, the vet? A very handsome man!

Yes, he is. — As far as this food goes ... I promise I'll pay you back tomorrow when Tom brings home his paycheck. Right now we don't have a penny to our names.

66 No money, no fun

For the last two months we've stayed home every single evening. Can't we go out at least once?

Go out? We still haven't got a penny to our names, and you want to waste money!

not to have a penny to one's name

keinen Pfennig mehr in der Tasche haben; keinen Pfennig sein Eigen nennen

(keinen Pfennig mehr in seinem Namen haben)

!

67

A business trip

You're going to Hawaii? But I thought you were broke. You still owe me for those eggs.

Listen, it's not a vacation. Tom has to go to Honolulu on business, and his boss said he could take me along. The only problem is the dog. We can't leave him here by himself, and we can't take him with us.

Forget it! No way! I'm not going to babysit your dog.

Oh, Anne, please. I know how much you love fresh pineapple, but you never buy it because it's so expensive. I also know that lots of delicious, juicy pineapples grow on Hawaii, and they don't cost an arm and a leg. Come on, I'm sure we can strike a bargain.

68

In a restaurant

Did you hear that? They don't take credit cards here. Only cash.

Uh-oh. I don't have any money on me. The credit card was our only chance.

What can we do now? You think they'll call the police?

No, I don't think so. We'll have to talk to the manager. I'm sure we can strike a bargain. Maybe we can wash dishes ...

!

to strike a bargain
etwas aushandeln; eine Abmachung treffen
(ein gutes Geschäft treffen)

69 A phone call

Hello.

Hello, Anne, this is Jane. How are you?

Jane? I thought you were in Honolulu.

I am, but I was worried about you and the dog. Is everything okay?

Well, so far he's only eaten three pairs of shoes. You'd better bring me lots of pineapples.

I will, I will. In fact, today I hit the jackpot: I went to a pineapple plantation and found the most delicious pineapples you've ever tasted.

70 Plain lucky

What!? You actually spent $ 800 on lottery tickets! You must be completely out of your mind.

But Sue Ellen, we could win 25 million dollars. This is the chance of a lifetime. I don't know what it is, but I have this strange feeling we're going to hit the jackpot.

to hit the jackpot
das große Los ziehen; Riesenerfolg haben
(den Jackpot treffen)

!

71 A dog of their own

Thanks for the pineapples, Jane, but I think you went a little overboard. You didn't have to bring me three whole suitcases full.

Well, they were so cheap, and I really appreciated your looking after the dog. I'm sure it wasn't a piece of cake.

Well, it wasn't in the beginning, but after a while he started growing on us. In fact, my husband liked him so much he said we should keep him.

Really? That would be great. I'll bring him back ...

Wait, I'm still thinking about it. You've said yourself a dog costs a lot, and he keeps getting into trouble. I'm not completely sold on the idea.

72 What if we won?

If we actually won all that money, we could finally go to Florida...

Florida? Why Florida? No, I wouldn't go there. It's not exclusive enough for millionaires like us.

What? All these years you've been talking about your «dream vacation». And now, all of a sudden, it's not good enough for you. Maybe I want to go now.

Fine, if we win, we'll go there first. I'm sorry, I simply didn't realize you were so sold on Florida.

!

to be sold on something
von einer Sache überzeugt/besessen sein
(an etwas verkauft sein)

73 A deal

You know, Ann, my husband is still unemployed. Even though he is very fond of the dog, we ...

We'll pay you to take the dog. One hundred dollars. Please! I can't stand that bag of fleas.

But, Ann, I couldn't take money from a friend ...

Yes, you can and you will. And I'll put my money where my mouth is right now. Here's a check for one hundred dollars.

74 Rich at last

Incredible, now that we've won 25 million, our worries are finally over.

Yes, and we can finally give some money to charities ...

To charities? Come on, we only won 25 million.

Hey, you were the one who was always preaching about helping the homeless, the poor, and the starving. I think it's time to put your money where your mouth is.

to put one's money where one's mouth is

Geld für frühere Versprechungen zur Verfügung stellen; den Worten (finanzielle) Taten folgen lassen (sein Geld dort hintun, wo der Mund ist)

!

WOOLWORTH
SPECIAL
!
HIRE AND FIRE
$52,000

75 A prowler

Oh, Ann, I'm really grateful that you let us have the dog. I feel guilty about taking your money. He's worth his weight in gold.

I consider it money well spent. What did he do to win you over?

Last night a prowler tried to break into our house, but the dog put a quick end to his plans. The guy ran for all he was worth, but the dog was faster. The dog caught him and bit him in the leg.

76 At home

It's not easy being rich. People we haven't heard from in years are writing us letters, calling us on the phone ...

... begging for money.

They're like vultures. As soon as they catch a glimpse of us, they chase after us for all they're worth.

for all one is worth
mit ganzer Kraft
(mit allem, was einer wert ist)

!

77 A picture in the newspaper

Jane, a journalist came to take a picture of our dog today! Did you see it the newspaper? He's a real hero.

Yeah, congratulations. The dog that's cracking down on crime.

And that's not all. Mr. Hooper who owns the jewelry store downtown called me after he read the story in the paper. He's been having a lot of problems with burglars lately, and he's willing to pay any price to get a good watchdog. He wants to buy our dog, and he said money is no object.

78 You're taking a big chance

You're going to invest in an oil firm that hasn't struck oil in years? That's so stupid! How much are you going to give them?

I've got a good feeling about this company. Something tells me they're going to strike oil soon, and they're going to strike it rich. They just need the right equipment and the right people. So I've told them to pay whatever was necessary to buy and hire the best. Money is no object.

!

Money is no object.
Geld spielt keine Rolle.
(Geld ist keine Sache.)

79 Nights only

I told Mr. Hooper we had become very attached to the dog and that we couldn't sell it. But I did agree to let him have it in the evenings — just until he catches his burglar. He's even paying us.
Hooper's actually renting your dog!? What a fool! He'd be better off investing his money in a good alarm system. That dog isn't going to scare away his burglar.
I wouldn't be so sure of that if I were you. That dog is really brave, and he can get vicious when he has to. Don't sell him short!

80 Oil!

I really thought you were throwing our money out of the window, J.R., but it looks like your company is a success. Ewing Oil is going to make millions. Everybody says this is the richest oil field in years.
I told you, Sue Ellen, never sell me short. Some people just have it.

to sell someone/something short
jemanden/etwas unterschätzen
(jemandem zu wenig fürs Geld geben)

!

TOPIC 4 VOCABULARY

61 A new house pet

pet
Haustier

to pee
pinkeln

to eat someone out of house and home
jemandem die Haare vom Kopf fressen; jemanden arm fressen

to let someone be the judge
jemanden selbst entscheiden lassen

to have a hard time
Schwierigkeiten haben

62 Home after work

I'm sick and tired of it.
Ich hab's satt.

to be out of the red
aus den roten Zahlen sein

to pay off
abbezahlen

to work one's fingers to the bone
sich kaputtarbeiten; sich die Finger wund arbeiten

63 A nosy neighbor

nosy
neugierig

to make a mess
Unordnung/Sauerei machen

divorce lawyer
Scheidungsanwalt

to waste time
Zeit verschwenden

to spread gossip
alles weitertratschen

64 A concerned friend

to pay off the mortgage
die Hypothek abbezahlen

It sets us back $30.
Das kostet uns $ 30.

65 Four eggs and a loaf of bread

stuff
Zeug(s)

not to have red cent
keinen roten Heller besitzen

vet
Tierarzt

handsome
gut aussehend (nur für Männer)

as far as ... goes
was ... anbetrifft

paycheck
Gehaltsscheck

66 No money, no fun

every single evening
jeden Abend

67 A business trip

broke
pleite

to babysit ...
auf ... aufpassen

pineapple
Ananas

juicy
saftig

to cost an arm and a leg
ein Heidengeld kosten

Come on!
Mach doch, gib dir 'nen Ruck!

68 In a restaurant

I don't have any money on me.
Ich habe kein Geld dabei.

to wash dishes
Geschirr spülen

69 A phone call

so far
bis jetzt

pineapple plantation
Ananasplantage

70 Plain lucky

to be plain lucky
einfach nur Glück haben

to be completely out of one's mind
völlig übergeschnappt sein

71 A dog of their own

to go overboard
es übertreiben

suitcase
Koffer

to appreciate something
etwas zu schätzen wissen; dankbar sein für

a piece of cake
siehe «Food and Drink» 27/28

to grow on someone
einem ans Herz wachsen

72 What if we won?

if we actually won
wenn wir tatsächlich gewinnen würden

all of a sudden
urplötzlich

73 A deal

unemployed
arbeitslos

to be fond of ...
... sehr gern haben; mögen

flea
Floh

bag of fleas
Ansammlung von Flöhen

74 Rich at last

rich at last
endlich reich

charity
Wohltätigkeitsverein

the homeless
die Obdachlosen

75 A prowler

prowler
Herumtreiber; Einbrecher

to feel guilty
ein schlechtes Gewissen haben

He is worth his weight in gold.
Er ist Gold wert; unbezahlbar

money well spent
gut angelegtes Geld

to win someone over
jemanden für sich gewinnen

to put an end to something
kurzen Prozess machen

76 At home

to beg for money
um Geld betteln

vulture
Geier

to catch a glimpse of something
einen flüchtigen Blick von ... erhaschen

to chase after
verfolgen

77 A picture in the newspaper

hero
Held

to crack down on
scharf vorgehen gegen

jewelry
Schmuck

burglar
Einbrecher

to pay any price
jeden Preis zahlen

watchdog
Wachhund

78 You're taking a big chance

to take a chance
ein Risiko eingehen

to strike oil
Öl finden

to strike it rich
überraschend zu Geld kommen

79 Nights only

to become attached to ...
... ins Herz schließen

to be better off
besser dran sein

I wouldn't be so sure of that if I were you.
Wenn ich du wäre, wäre ich mir dessen nicht so sicher.

vicious
bösartig

80 Oil!

to throw money out of the window
Geld zum Fenster rausschmeißen

Some people just have it.
Einige wissen eben, wie man's anstellt.

1. What's the best answer?

1. Michael's parents gave him a thousand dollars for his birthday. He really
- **a** hit the jackpot.
- **b** doesn't have a penny to his name.
- **c** put his money where his mouth is.

2. You say you want to help the poor, but words aren't enough. Why don't you
- **a** put your money where your mouth is?
- **b** sell them short?
- **c** strike a bargain?

3. I don't care how much it costs. I want it,
- **a** I'll mind my own business.
- **b** money is no object.
- **c** I don't have a penny to my name.

4. This doesn't concern you. You should
- **a** make ends meet.
- **b** mind your own business.
- **c** strike a bargain.

5. You know I don't earn very much. You'll have to spend less on food and clothes, if we are going to
- **a** hit the jackpot.
- **b** be sold on this.
- **c** make ends meet.

6. You said you'd give me five dollars if I swallowed the goldfish. Well, I swallowed it, so
- **a** you don't have a penny to your name.
- **b** money is no object.
- **c** put your money where your mouth is.

2. Say it using an idiom

1. Don't underestimate him! He can do it!

2. I have to find him. It doesn't matter how much it costs.

3. We are finding it very difficult to pay all of our bills with the money we earn.

4. This doesn't concern him.

5. You said you'd buy me a new dress, so now you'd better give me the money like you promised.

6. Frank has absolutely no money.

7. I think Alice is really enthusiastic about spending a week in the Caribbean.

8. When the dog started barking, he ran as fast and as far as he possibly could.

9. Don't go. I'm certain we can reach an agreement.

10. You were very, very lucky when you married that girl. She's perfect.

3. Match the phrases

1. John doesn't approve of your plan, he isn't…
2. Okay, I won't ask any more questions. I know when I should…
3. We have to finish making dinner before he gets here. We've got to…
4. You have never believed in him. You have always…
5. We're going to the most expensive restaurant in the city. Tonight…
6. Instead of just talking about having the car fixed, you should…
7. You want to buy this and I want to sell it. I'm sure that eventually we'll be able to…
8. Since my wife also got a job, we're finding it easier to…
9. He can't buy new clothes or find a place to live, because he doesn't…
10. Three women want to marry you? It sounds like you…

- **a.** …money is no object.
- **b.** …sold on it.
- **c.** …have a penny to his name.
- **d.** …put your money where your mouth is.
- **e.** …work for all we're worth.
- **f.** …strike a bargain.
- **g.** …hit the jackpot.
- **h.** …make ends meet.
- **i.** …sold him short.
- **j.** …mind my own business.

Answers: 1. ☐ 2. ☐ 3. ☐ 4. ☐ 5. ☐ 6. ☐ 7. ☐ 8. ☐ 9. ☐ 10. ☐

4. Translate

1. Ich habe keinen Pfennig mehr in der Tasche.

....

....

2. Ich habe mit ganzer Kraft zurückgeschlagen.

....

....

3. Wir werden irgendwie etwas aushandeln.

....

....

4. Ich bin von diesem Plan überzeugt.

....

....

5. Glaube mir, Geld spielt keine Rolle.

....

....

6. Wir kommen finanziell nicht über die Runden.

....

....

7. Wir sollten uns um unsere eigenen Angelegenheiten kümmern.

....

....

8. Wir haben ihn unterschätzt.

....

....

9. Du solltest den Worten Taten folgen lassen.

....

....

10. Ich habe das große Los gezogen.

....

....

TOPIC 5

NATURE

81 A case of mistaken identity

Hello, darling, I've been waiting for you for hours.

Excuse me, are you talking to me?

Oh, Samuel, up to your tricks again? Pretending you don't know me?

But I don't know you, miss. There must be some kind of misunderstanding. You're mistaking me for someone else.

Really, dear, we don't have time for your silly games. If we don't hurry, we'll miss our flight. Remember, tonight's our wedding night.

Wedding night? Listen, I've never seen you before in my life. You're very attractive, and I'm reluctant to nip these ideas about marriage in the bud, but I'm leaving. Good-bye!

82 The land of Oz

That's it. I'm going to Australia this winter!

Are you certain you want to spend your holiday in Australia? I always wanted to go there too — until I read a little about it. It's too hot, they have all kinds of poisonous snakes there, and the ozone hole is right above Tasmania. I'm sorry, but that article in the newspaper about the skin cancer rate in Australia nipped all my enthusiasm in the bud.

to nip something in the bud
etwas im Keim ersticken
(schon in der Knospe abbrechen)

!

83 A torrent of tears

But wh-wh-why? Wh-wh-what did I do wrong?
Hey, let go of me and stop crying! People are looking at us. They'll think I'm trying to rob you or something. Here take my handkerchief.
Are you ha-ha-having an affair with another woman?
Lady, take a deep breath and calm down. I'm too old for this kind of excitement. I am not involved with you or any other woman. I haven't looked at a woman in years. Old men like me don't sow their wild oats anymore.

84 Thailand

What about Thailand? Maybe I should spend my holiday there.
Have you gone completely mad? Do you want to catch malaria? Or hepatitis? Or AIDS?
I hate to disappoint you, but I'm not going there to sow my wild oats. I'm more interested in Buddhist temples than massage parlors.

!

to sow one's wild oats
sich die Hörner abstoßen; über die Stränge schlagen (seinen wilden Hafer säen)

85 A gunman

I'm sorry I made such a scene. Will you ever be able to forgive me?

Forgive you for what? I don't even know you.

Samuel, did you take your pills today? I think your memory is acting up again.

Listen, there's nothing wrong with my memory. I may be old, but all the parts are still in good working order. I'm more inclined to believe that y-o-u need the doctor.

Oh my God, there he is. He did follow me. Quick, if you want to live, get in this taxi or...

Hey, is that guy shooting at us?

Yes! Now, get in this taxi. We've got to get to the airport. If we miss that plane, we'll be up the creek without a paddle.

86 Bangkok

I decided that I wanted to go on holiday by myself, so I told my wife I'm going to Thailand this winter. Alone.

How did she take it?

Not too well. Right away she jumped to conclusions and assumed I only want to indulge in sexual adventures with Asian women. She was so angry she threw three plates and a couple of coffee cups at me.

Uh-oh. You're really up the creek.

to be up the creek (without a paddle)
in Schwierigkeiten stecken, ohne dass sich eine Lösung anbietet
(gegen den Strom ohne Paddel)

!

87

A bad day

Driver, get us to the airport and make it fast! There's an extra hundred dollars in it for you if you can lose the car that's following us.

Hell, I wish I'd never gotten out of bed this morning. First, I lose my wallet on the bus. Then a beautiful lunatic mistakes me for her fiancé, and I almost get shot while she's standing right next to me. Cripes, it never rains but it pours.

88

Back from the trip

Hi, Mark. How was Bangkok?

Not bad, except that the airline lost my luggage, my money was stolen, and the hotel was a dump.

It never rains but it pours.

!

It never rains but it pours.

Ein Unglück kommt selten allein.

(Es regnet nicht bloß, es schüttet gleich.)

NEW YORK TIMES

89 A henchman

Samuel, I insist you stop playing games with me. You are Samuel Meyer, professor of English literature, and I am going to marry you today in Las Vegas.
Wrong. My name is Harry Henderson. I'm a retired school teacher, and I've never seen you before today.
Oh, Samuel, you must be having one of your memory lapses again.
It's not my memory I'm worried about now. Who the heck is trying to kill me?
I'm sure it's one of my father's henchmen. I thought I managed to keep everything a secret, but it looks like Daddy Dear got wind of our elopement and decided to put an end to it.

90 Mark's wife

How are things at home? Is your wife still angry with you?
Well, as a matter of fact, she's not even home. While I was planning my trip, she must have been secretly getting ready for a trip of her own. She never mentioned it, but I found out anyway.
How?
I got wind of it when I called home and the neighbor that was watering our plants answered the phone.

!

to get wind of something
von einer Sache Wind bekommen

91 A missing wallet

Oh, Samuel, I wish I knew who spilled the beans ...

Stop calling me Samuel. My name is Harry.

Sure it is. If that's the case, show me some ID.

I can't. I lost my wallet on the bus, but there has to be some way to convince you.

Relax and save your energy. We have to get on that airplane.

Not me. I don't even know you.

That might be the case, but the man with the gun knows you. My father sent him to kill you, and that's exactly what he intends to do. He'll do everything to find us. He'll leave no stone unturned.

92 Where is Mark's wife?

So where did she go?

I wish I knew.

Maybe she just went to visit her mother. That's what women usually do.

No, not Carrie. She wouldn't do that, because her mother's been dead for ten years.

So what are you going to do? Just sit and wait?

Oh no, I'm going to search our apartment. There must be some clues that will help me find her, and I'll leave no stone unturned until I find them.

to leave no stone unturned
nichts unversucht lassen
(keinen Stein an Ort und Stelle lassen)

93 A birthmark

So you won't be safe till we're married. I just wish I could find a way to snap you out of this spell.
Hey, I know. Your birthmark!
Birthmark? What birthmark?
The birthmark on the back of your left thigh.
I don't have any such birthmark.
I'll believe that when I see it. Drop your pants.
My pants? Here in this taxi?
Yes, don't you want to prove to me that you're not Samuel?
Yes, but I don't know you, I, uh, I ...
Well, are you going to drop your pants or not? Yes or no? Stop beating around the bush.

94 She's back

I heard your wife's back.
That's right.
Did she tell you where she went? What happened?
Well ... she ...
Yes?
She ... she went on a trip.
I know that. But where did she go? Stop beating around the bush and give me a straight answer!

!

to beat around/about the bush
nicht zur Sache kommen; wie die Katze um den heißen Brei herumschleichen; Umschweife machen
(um den Busch herumschlagen)

95 A prude

Well?

Hold on a minute. Get your hands off that zipper, young lady!

You have to take off your pants. It's the only way to settle this once and for all.

Yes, but I can unzip my own pants. I know you young people nowadays are more casual about things like that, but I'm a man, I've always worn the pants in my house, and I'm the one who takes them off. I'm not going to allow any woman to undress me, especially not one who could be my granddaughter.

Oh, Samuel, you're such a stick-in-the-mud.

96 The mystery remains

Oh, I get it! You still don't know where she went.

That's right, I don't. She just won't tell me. In a way I'm still amazed she took off on her own. She never wanted to go anywhere alone, she always wanted to stay at home. This is so unlike her, she was always such a stick-in-the-mud.

a stick-in-the-mud
jemand, der keine Lust auf etwas Neues hat; Rückschrittler; Tranfunzel
(ein Stock im Schlamm)

!

97 A vow

It's not there. No birthmark!

I told you so.

Then you really aren't Samuel ... I don't understand. You're a dead ringer for him, and your voice. That's Samuel's voice.

Well, I've heard stories about things like this. Lots of people think there's a person somewhere on the planet that looks just like each of us.

But where is Samuel? What happened to him?

I haven't got the faintest idea, and I don't really care. I just want to get out of this taxi and go home.

But you can't! I already told you: My father swore he'd kill any man who tried to marry me, and believe me, come hell or high water, Daddy's henchmen always get their man.

98 Suspicion

She's still a beautiful woman. Did it ever occur to you that she might be having an affair, and that she and her lover went on that trip together?

Yes, it did and believe me, I'm going to find out what really happened, come hell or high water.

!

come hell or high water

ganz gleich, welche Schwierigkeiten auch überwunden werden müssen

(ganz gleich, ob Hölle oder Hochwasser kommt)

99 Lots of trouble

We're almost at the airport, and I haven't seen his car. Hopefully we lost him.

God, I hope so. What are we going to do?

Well, I'm still going to Las Vegas, and you'd better come with me. I'll try to contact Samuel when we get there. Oh, God, I hope he's all right.

What if he isn't? What if ... ?

Don't even think that. Samuel'd better be all right and he'd better marry me tonight, or we'll really be in hot water. My father would send a whole army out after you if ...

An army?! You mean that guy with the gun is o-n-l-y the tip of the iceberg?

100 Psychological help

Well, Mark, I don't really know what went wrong between you two. When you went to Thailand, she went somewhere else. She gave you a dose of your own medicine, but she hasn't told you anything about it. I really think that your marital problems run much deeper. Her taking off on her own was just the tip of the iceberg.

the tip of the iceberg
die Spitze des Eisbergs

81 A case of mistaken identity

mistaken identity
Verwechslung (zweier Personen)

for hours
stundenlang

to be up to one's tricks
Dummheiten machen; seine alte Schau/Nummer abziehen

to pretend
vorgeben; vortäuschen

I'm reluctant
es widerstrebt mir

82 The land of Oz

the land of Oz
scherzhaft für Australien

skin cancer rate
Hautkrebshäufigkeit

83 A torrent of tears

torrent
Sturzbach

Let go of me.
Lass mich los.

to take a deep breath
einmal tief durchatmen

to be involved
mit jemandem eine Beziehung haben

84 Thailand

hepatitis
Gelbsucht

massage parlor
Massagesalon; Bordell

85 A gunman

gunman
Killer

to act up again
wieder loslegen; wieder Schwierigkeiten machen

in good working order
in funktionstüchtigem Zustand

to be inclined to believe
geneigt sein zu glauben

86 Bangkok

How did she take it?
Wie hat sie's aufgenommen?

to jump to conclusions
voreilige Schlüsse ziehen

to indulge in ...
... frönen; sich ... hingeben

87 A bad day

there's ... in it for you
du kannst dir ... dazuverdienen

to lose the car
den Wagen abschütteln

lunatic
Wahnsinnige/r

fiancé
Verlobter

Cripes!
Herr im Himmel!

88 Back from the trip

dump
ein mieses Loch (Schutthalde)

89 A henchman

henchman
gedungener Killer

to play games with
mit jemandem sein Spielchen treiben

memory lapse
Gedächtnislücke

who the heck
wer zum Teufel

elopement
Durchbrennen, um gegen den Willen der Eltern zu heiraten

to put an end to
beenden

90 Mark's wife

How are things at home?
Wie läuft's zu Hause?

91 A missing wallet

to spill the beans
siehe «Food and Drink» 21/22

to be the case
zutreffen; der Fall sein

ID
Ausweis

to intend
vorhaben

92 Where is Mark's wife?

I wish I knew.
Ich wünschte, ich wüsste es.

to sit and wait
in aller Ruhe abwarten

clue
Hinweis

93 A birthmark

birthmark
Muttermal

to snap someone out of something
jemanden aus etwas «herausholen» (z. B. aus einer miesen Laune)

spell
Verwirrung; Zauber

thigh
Schenkel

to drop one's pants
seine Hosen runterlassen

94 She's back

to give a straight answer
ohne Umschweife antworten

95 A prude

prude
prüder Typ

zipper
Reißverschluss

to settle something once and for all
eine Sache ein für alle Mal aus der Welt schaffen; etwas klarstellen

to wear the pants in one's house
zu Hause die Hosen anhaben

96 The mystery remains

I get it!
Jetzt kapier ich's!

to take off
abhauen

This is so unlike her.
Das sieht ihr so gar nicht ähnlich.

97 A vow

vow
Schwur; Gelöbnis

I told you so.
Hab ich dir doch gleich gesagt.

a dead ringer
Doppelgänger

I haven't got the faintest idea.
Ich habe nicht die leiseste Ahnung.

98 Suspicion

Did it ever occur to you that ...
Ist es dir je in den Sinn gekommen, dass ...

99 Lots of trouble

you'd (= had) better come
du tätest gut daran, mitzukommen

to be in hot water
ganz schön Probleme haben; in Teufels Küche sein

She gave you a dose of your own medicine.
Sie hat dich mit deinen eigenen Waffen geschlagen.

to run much deeper
tiefere Ursachen haben

TOPIC 5 EXERCISES

1. What's the best answer?

1. We must find my keys! I will
- **a** sow my wild oats.
- **b** be a stick-in-the-mud.
- **c** leave no stone unturned.

2. I'm sure we'll find more corrupt politicians in this city,
- **a** this is just the tip of the iceberg.
- **b** we shouldn't beat around the bush.
- **c** we should get wind of this.

3. Smoking is a very bad habit. You should
- **a** beat around the bush.
- **b** nip it in the bud.
- **c** smoke, come hell or high water.

4. If Mom finds out that we broke it, she'll be very angry. We'll
- **a** get wind of it.
- **b** be up the creek without a paddle.
- **c** beat around the bush.

5. My husband never wants to try anything new,
- **a** he's a stick-in-the-mud.
- **b** he likes sowing his wild oats.
- **c** he'll leave no stone unturned.

6. I promise that I will always help you,
- **a** it's the tip of the iceberg.
- **b** it never rains but it pours.
- **c** come hell or high water.

2. Say it using an idiom

1. The police will do everything possible to find the missing child.

2. Whenever I ask him, he avoids giving me a definite answer.

3. How did you find out about my plans?

4. My mother is very old-fashioned and refuses to try new things.

5. A disaster is often followed by other disasters.

6. No matter what happens, I will always love you.

7. We are in a lot of trouble.

8. This is only a small part of much larger problem.

9. Young men want to do foolish things and sleep with lots of women before they get married.

10. We have to put an end to this drug problem before it gets worse.

3. Match the phrases

1. Hector's going to kill you when he finds out, you'll be…
2. Don't worry, your fiancé will return after he…
3. He hates anything new or different. He's such…
4. Kevin has a lot of problems. The drugs you found in his pocket are just…
5. Alan never says yes or no. He always…
6. Don't worry, Debbie'll never find out. She'll never…
7. You shouldn't let the dog bark at small children, you have to…
8. I'll never leave her side for a minute. I'll stay with her,…
9. He looked everywhere for the lost money. He…
10. I lost my job and then my house burned down,…

- **a.** … it never rains but it pours.
- **b.** … a stick-in-the-mud.
- **c.** … left no stone unturned.
- **d.** … the tip of the iceberg.
- **e.** … nip this bad behavior in the bud.
- **f.** … beats around the bush.
- **g.** … come hell or high water.
- **h.** … get wind of it.
- **i.** … sows his wild oats.
- **j.** … up the creek without a paddle.

Answers: 1. ☐ 2. ☐ 3. ☐ 4. ☐ 5. ☐ 6. ☐ 7. ☐ 8. ☐ 9. ☐ 10. ☐

4. Translate

1. Ein Unglück kommt selten allein.

....

....

2. Du musst das Problem im Keim ersticken.

....

....

3. Sie macht mich echt wütend. Sie kommt einfach nicht zur Sache.

....

....

4. Wie hat er Wind davon bekommen?

....

....

5. Mein Mann ist ein echter Langweiler.

....

....

6. Bernie muss sich die Hörner abstoßen.

....

....

7. Wir werden nichts unversucht lassen.

....

....

8. Du wirst es schaffen, egal welche Schwierigkeiten du auch überwinden musst.

....

....

9. Er steckt bis über beide Ohren in Schwierigkeiten.

....

....

10. Das ist nur die Spitze des Eisbergs.

....

....

TOPIC 6

TIME

101 5:30 a.m.

Wake up, sleepy head! Rise and shine! It's already 5:30.

5:30 in the morning! Have you lost your mind?

Julia, you promised to go bird-watching with me today and I've got my heart set on it.

When I made that promise, you didn't tell me I'd have to get up so early. Oh, Ralph, you know I hate walking around in the forest with all the flies and mosquitoes. Besides, you must be exhausted. You didn't come to bed until after three.

3:35 to be exact, but I'm as fit as a fiddle. I wanted to read through all the books I have on birds and memorize all the names. That meant I had to burn the midnight oil.

102 At a garage

Well, Mr. Simpson, you need a new muffler. The old one is badly rusted and it's got a big hole in it.

All right. When will it be ready?

In about two or three days.

Three days?! You're pulling my leg! I'm only traveling through. I have to be in Detroit tomorrow night.

I'm sorry, but we don't have any mufflers in stock. I have to order one. If you're really lucky, we'll get it by five or six this afternoon.

Great! Then I can have my car back by tomorrow morning.

Yeah, but I'll have to burn the midnight oil to install it — which will cost you a bit extra.

to burn the midnight oil
bis in die Puppen (tief in die Nacht) arbeiten
(Mitternachtsöl verbrennen)

103 **5:35 a.m.**
Come on, it's going to be a beautiful day.
How can you be sure? It's still pitch black out there.
I listened to the weather report on the radio: fair skies and moderate temperatures. Perfect weather for bird-watching. And I even made liverwurst sandwiches for you. Your favorite!
Liverwurst sandwiches? With spicy mustard?
Of course, I made them just the way you like them.
All right. I can't say no to liverwurst. I'm getting up.
Thanks, honey. Beautiful weather and a beautiful wife beside me. This really makes my day.

104 **Later the same day, on the telephone**
Mr. Simpson, the new muffler's arrived. We'll have your car ready in the morning.
Great! Fantastic. You've made my day.

!

to make one's day
jemanden glücklich machen; jemandes Tag retten (jemandes Tag machen)

105 **6:10 a.m.**

Well, how do you feel now? Did the shower help?

My eyes are open, but I desperately need a cup of coffee.

There's a whole thermos of hot coffee waiting for you in the car. Let's go.

If you insist.

Cheer up! We're going to have a great time and ...

A great time? I'm going to get hot and sweaty, and the mosquitoes are going to eat me alive. I'll probably fall down a couple of times and break some of my fingernails. That doesn't sound like my idea of a good time.

You're such a pessimist! Look on the bright side: We'll be out together in the fresh air and sunshine. You're really going to enjoy yourself.

Me? Enjoy myself? That'll be the day!

106 **Several hours later**

Mr. Simpson, sorry I have to bother you again, but we're having a little problem with your car. The muffler's been installed, but now we're having problems with the carburetor. You want us to fix that too?

If it's absolutely necessary, I have no objections — as long as I can still pick up the car tomorrow morning! You c-a-n fix it, can't you?

Us not being able to fix a car? That'll be the day!

That'll be the day!
Nie im Leben! Das ist äußerst unwahrscheinlich.
(Das wird der Tag sein!)

107 8:40 a.m.

Gee, I told you it was going to be a beautiful day.
All right, for once the weatherman was right. But it isn't much fun sitting in the car, looking at it through the window. We've been driving around for hours. Are you sure you know where you're going?
Of course, I do. Gee, Julia, you're worse than a little kid. Have some patience. You don't have to go to the bathroom, do you?
No, but I'm sick and tired of sitting here. How much longer? When are we going to get there?
All in good time. Sit back and relax.

108 Early the next morning

Oh, Mr. Simpson, here already? I'm sorry, but your car isn't ready yet ...
You're not done? But yesterday you promised...
I know, but when I called I didn't know we had to replace the entire carburetor. That took a few hours. And then this morning we discovered the ignition has a slight glitch, so now we have to take care of that too.
This is a nightmare. When can I finally have my car back?
You'll have it all in good time. Why don't you get yourself some breakfast first? Come back in an hour.

!

all in good time
alles zu seiner Zeit; eins nach dem anderen
(alles in guter Zeit)

109 9:05 a.m.

Look over there. See that sign? Mount Field National Park.

Is this it?

Yes.

You mean we're finally here? I can get out of the car and stretch my legs?

Yes. Don't get so excited. We've only ...

Finally! Five minutes more in this car and I would have hit you over the head, thrown you in the back seat, and headed for home. You're lucky I didn't have to get violent.

Oooh, sounds like you were getting really impatient. I guess we got here in the nick of time.

110 After breakfast

Ah, Mr. Simpson, back so early? How was your breakfast?

Stop beating around the bush! Is the car ready or not?

Not really. We found out why the ignition wasn't working properly. Somebody had been tampering with your car. We found an explosive device connected to the ignition, set to explode at 10:05 a.m. We managed to defuse it at ten o'clock, just in the nick of time. Otherwise it would've blown us all to high heaven.

in the nick of time
keine Sekunde zu spät; gerade noch rechtzeitig (innerhalb der Zeitmarke)

!

111 11:00 a.m.

Over there, oh my God, it's a black cockatoo!
Where? Where? I don't see anything.
Fantastic! Up there in that big tree ...
Ralph, we're in the forest! There are trees all over the place. Listen, I'm tired of walking, and I think these boots are giving me blisters. Why don't you go on alone? I'll sit down here on this rock and wait for you.
But Julia, what will you do here by yourself? You'll get bored.
Oh no, I won't. I'm always prepared. Where are my ... I'm sure I put them in my pack. Ah, here they are. I'll just ...
A file and some fingernail polish? You're going to give yourself a manicure in the middle of the woods?
Why not? It'll keep me busy for a while. It's a perfect way to kill time.

112 Mr. Simpson has had it

But now everything is okay. You can have your car back in an hour or so.
Well, I don't want to sound ungrateful, but I'm getting a little impatient. You're telling me all kinds of strange things about my car. Sure, the muffler was old — but who on earth would want to kill me with a car bomb?
I don't know. Maybe your wife ...
I'm single!
Listen, Mr. Simpson, why don't you go back to the Roadhouse Café and kill some time there? I'll have the car ready in an hour.

!

to kill time
Zeit totschlagen
(Zeit töten)

113

2:10 p.m.

Yoo-hoo! Julia? Where are you?
Ralph? Over here! Ralph?
Hi, honey. You wouldn't believe how many beautiful ...
Ralph! Do you know what time it is?
No, I forgot to put my watch on this morning. I don't know, maybe twelve o'clock.
Twelve? It's after two. I was getting ready to send out a search party to find you. You've been gone for over three hours.
Three hours? Really? It seems like I left you just a minute ago. Time flies when you're having fun.

114

Simpson makes a phone call

If you need to use the phone, be my guest. It's the least I can do for you, Mr. Simpson.
Thanks. — Hello? Hello? Hi, hi, this is Pete, Pete Simpson. I'm sorry I won't make it in time for our appointment. My car broke down, and the local mechanic seems to be totally incompetent ... Where am I? In the middle of nowhere, it's a small town called Oskaloosa. I've been stuck in this lousy place for one and a half days now. I'm telling you, time flies when you're having fun.

Time flies when you're having fun.
Die Zeit vergeht wie im Fluge, wenn man sich amüsiert.
[Oft ironisch gebraucht.]
(Die Zeit fliegt, wenn man Spaß hat.)

!

WALL STREET

115 2:15 p.m.

I'm sorry. I didn't mean to worry you, I just lost track of time. This place is full of the most amazing birds. I saw three ...
Stop right there! If you start talking about birds, I'll never get out of here. I want to go home. The sun's disappeared, and those clouds are getting darker by the minute. Ralph, let's go home.
Don't let a couple of clouds spoil the fun. Unpack the sandwiches and let's have a picnic. The wind will blow those clouds away in a few minutes and the sun'll come back out. I'm sure it won't rain to...
Oh no! Looks like you spoke too soon. It's raining. Run!

116 The finishing touches

Almost there. Just one more screw to tighten. Oops. I spoke too soon. I must have hit the tank, now it's leaking.

to speak too soon
den Tag vor dem Abend loben; etwas vorschnell als sicher darstellen
(zu voreilig sprechen)

!

117

3:30 p.m.

Julia, please! Please say something. I'm sorry, but this trip wasn't really that bad ...

It wasn't that bad!? It was miserable. First, you dragged me out of bed at an ungodly hour and forced me to tramp through the woods looking for stupid birds. Then you go off and desert me and when you finally come back, it starts raining cats and dogs. You take off and run to the car, leaving me behind again. When I try to catch up with you, I slip in the mud and fall down, breaking three fingernails. Now I'm cold and wet and hungry. That doesn't sound like a lot of fun to me.

Enough, enough. You're right. You've had a lot of bad experiences today. I'm sorry. This certainly hasn't been your day.

118

The mechanic screws up again

I'm sorry, Mr. Simpson. I didn't mean to puncture the tank with my screwdriver. When I tried to tighten that last screw, the screwdriver slipped and it poked right into the tank. I'm really sorry about this. Nothing's going right. This is not my day.

!

not to be one's day

einen schlechten Tag haben
(nicht jemandes Tag sein)

119 5:30 p.m.

Feel better now?

Yes, I think I've finally dried out, and this steak is delicious.

Almost finished?

Yes.

Good, I'll get the bill.

What's the big hurry?

I can't wait to get home and look up all the birds I saw today in my books. I think I saw some really rare ones ...

Oh, Ralph, don't you ever get enough?

I tell you, Julia, that place is full of birds. When do you think we can go there again?

I think you're going to have a long wait. I'll go bird-watching again when hell freezes over.

120 The bill

Well, Mr. Simpson, that wasn't that bad, was it? Your car is as good as new. Now let's see. One muffler, a new carburetor, ignition and a new tank... plus labor, of course. That comes to $ 3000. Cash or credit card?

$ 3000?! For such a lousy job? Ha! I'll pay you that much when hell freezes over.

when hell freezes over
nie und nimmer
(wenn die Hölle zufriert)

!

101 5:30 a.m.

sleepy head
Schlafmütze

Rise and shine!
Steh auf!
Wörtlich: Steh auf und scheine!

to lose one's mind
seinen Verstand verlieren

I've got my heart set on it.
Mein Herz hängt daran.

to be fit as a fiddle
putzmunter (fit wie eine Fiedel)

to memorize
auswendig lernen

102 At a garage

muffler
Auspuff

to pull someone's leg
siehe «The Human Body» 51/52

to travel through
auf der Durchreise sein

to have ... in stock
... auf Lager haben

103 5:35 a.m.

pitch black
pechschwarz

your favorite
dein Lieblingsessen

mustard
Senf

104 Later the same day, on the telephone

to arrive
ankommen

105 6:10 a.m.

desperately
unbedingt

Cheer up!
Sei nicht so verbissen!

to eat someone alive
jemanden bei lebendigem Leibe auffressen

to look on the bright side
auch die guten Seiten sehen

106 Several hours later

carburetor
Vergaser

objection
Einwand

107 8:40 a.m.

weatherman
TV-Meteorologe

Gee!
Mensch! Mann!

to have to go to the bathroom
aufs Klo müssen

to be sick and tired of something
etwas wirklich satt haben

108 Early the next morning

You're not done?
Sie sind noch nicht fertig?

ignition
Zündanlage

glitch
Macke; Fehler

109 9:05 a.m.

to stretch one's legs
sich die Beine vertreten

to head for ...
Richtung ... fahren

violent
gewalttätig

impatient
ungeduldig

110 After breakfast

to beat around the bush
siehe «Nature» 93/94

to tamper with ...
sich an ... zu schaffen machen

explosive device
explosives Gerät (Bombe)

to defuse
entschärfen

to blow to high heaven
in die Luft sprengen

111 11:00 a.m.

cockatoo
Kakadu

all over the place
überall

blister
Blase (an den Füßen)

file
Nagelfeile

fingernail polish
Nagellack

112 Mr. Simpson has had it

He's had it.
Jetzt reicht's ihm aber.

ungrateful
undankbar

113 2:10 p.m.

search party
Suchtrupp

114 Simpson makes a phone call

Be my guest.
siehe «Odds and Ends» 159/160

the least I can do
das Mindeste, was ich tun kann

appointment
Termin; Verabredung

in the middle of nowhere
am Ende der Welt; in einer gottverlassenen Gegend

to be stuck
festsitzen

115 2:15 p.m.

to lose track of something
etwas aus den Augen verlieren; nicht mehr an etwas denken

to spoil
verderben

116 The finishing touches

Almost there!
Gleich haben wir's!

to tighten
anziehen; festziehen

to leak
leck sein

117 3:30 p.m.

to drag
schleppen

ungodly hour
unchristlich frühe Stunde

to desert
verlassen

to rain cats and dogs
in Strömen gießen

to catch up with someone
jemanden einholen

to slip in the mud
im Schlamm ausrutschen

118 The mechanic screws up again

to screw up
Mist bauen; sich einen Patzer leisten

to puncture
durchstechen; ein Loch machen

screwdriver
Schraubenzieher

to poke
piksen; stechen

119 5:30 p.m.

rare
selten; rar

a long wait
eine lange Wartezeit

120 The bill

as good as new
so gut wie neu

labor
Arbeitslohn

that comes to ...
das macht (kostet) ...

lousy job
äußerst dürftige Leistung

TOPIC 6 EXERCISES

1. What's the best answer?

1. I'll n-e-v-e-r tell you the secret. You'll get the information from me

- **a** in the nick of time.
- **b** all in good time.
- **c** when hell freezes over.

2. He's really tired this morning, because

- **a** time flies when you're having fun.
- **b** he had to burn the midnight oil.
- **c** he spoke too soon.

3. Me pass an examination? No, I'm too stupid,

- **a** that'll be the day!
- **b** all in good time.
- **c** in the nick of time.

4. Today I lost my job and my wife walked out on me,

- **a** all in good time.
- **b** in the nick of time.
- **c** this isn't my day.

5. I guess we'll have to wait a long time. What can we do to

- **a** burn the midnight oil?
- **b** kill time?
- **c** make our day?

6. He almost died, but the ambulance arrived

- **a** in the nick of time.
- **b** when hell freezes over.
- **c** all in good time.

2. Say it using an idiom

1. I'm sure she'll find something to do to fill up the time while she's waiting.

2. Now that exams are right around the corner, a lot of students are staying up late, studying.

3. You said something would happen but just the opposite occurred.

4. I will n-e-v-e-r get into an airplane.

5. Your phone call made me very happy today.

6. Today everything I do goes wrong, it's a terrible day.

7. Richard g-e-t married? That is very unlikely.

8. Time passes by very quickly when you are doing something you enjoy.

9. You want me to do my homework? Not now, later.

10. He jumped from in front of the train at the last possible moment.

3. Match the phrases

1. There's nothing I want to do more than hit you in the face, so please start a fight with me and…
2. That tree almost fell on me. You pushed me out of the way just…
3. Send a man to Mars? I don't think so,…
4. I wish I had never got out of bed this morning. This…
5. If you want to finish this before the meeting tomorrow morning, you'll have to…
6. I'm not doing anything special, just…
7. You were wrong about her, she's very nice. When you said she was unfriendly, you…
8. I hate you. I'll go out with you…
9. I can't believe it's already five o'clock. Boy, you were right when you said…
10. You just have to wait a little longer. You'll hear the results…

a. …all in good time.
b. …burn the midnight oil.
c. …time flies when you're having fun.
d. …that'll be the day.
e. …spoke too soon.
f. …make my day.
g. …hasn't been my day.
h. …in the nick of time.
i. …when hell freezes over.
j. …killing time.

Answers: 1. ☐ 2. ☐ 3. ☐ 4. ☐ 5. ☐ 6. ☐ 7. ☐ 8. ☐ 9. ☐ 10. ☐

4. Translate

1. Dieses Geschenk hat mich glücklich gemacht.

....

....

2. Du hast den Tag vor dem Abend gelobt.

....

....

3. Du bist gerade noch rechtzeitig gekommen.

....

....

4. Das ist äußerst unwahrscheinlich!

....

....

5. Ich werde dich niemals küssen.

....

....

6. Die Zeit vergeht wie im Fluge, wenn einem etwas Spaß macht.

....

....

7. Wenn ich das fertig kriegen will, muss ich bis tief in die Nacht arbeiten.

....

....

8. Heute habe ich einen schlechten Tag.

....

....

9. Womit können wir die Zeit totschlagen?

....

....

10. Alles zu seiner Zeit.

....

....

TOPIC 7

UTENSILS & TOOLS

121 Charlie's mother

Uh, Mom, would you mind moving that box? It's right in front of the television.

Charlie, are you deaf? I told you to turn that thing off five minutes ago. I need your help.

Aw, Mom, now? This is really an interesting show ...

Fat men dressed up in silly costumes pretending to wrestle? You think that's interesting?

Yeah, what's wrong with wrestling? Dad likes it.

Don't remind me. You and your father both waste too much time in front of the TV. I was hoping you wouldn't pick up his bad habits, but it looks like you're a chip off the old block.

122 At the Argyle School for Young Men

Mason Devonport's in the headmaster's office again.

Really? Well, he's in my algebra lesson this morning, and I'd rather he stayed away. It's impossible to get anything accomplished with that rowdy in the classroom.

Yes, Mason's always in trouble, and it doesn't surprise me at all when you consider who his father is. Robert Devonport was the most obnoxious rascal, always disrupting my Latin lessons and forever getting into some mischief. It appears young Mason is a chip off the old block.

a chip off the old block
ganz (wie) der Vater
(ein Splitter vom alten Block)

!

123 A box of old clothes

Are you satisfied now?

Yes, thanks for switching that nonsense off. This won't take long.

I hope not. A movie I've been dying to see starts at 2 o'clock.

Okay, let's get down to business. — Here, try this on.

This? Where did you get this, the Salvation Army?

No, these are some of your older brother's things. He wore them when he was your age. I think they'll fit you.

You've got to be kidding. You actually want me to wear Joe's old rags?

Exactly! You've hit the nail on the head.

124 In the dining hall

Please pass the salt ... where is the salt shaker?

The kitchen staff had to remove them before they started serving lunch. Apparently someone sneaked into the dining hall this morning and unscrewed all the lids on the salt shakers. When the headmaster tried to sprinkle some salt on his mashed potatoes, he got more than he bargained for. You should have seen his face.

Sounds like one of Mason Devonport's pranks ...

You've hit the nail on the head. He's sitting in the headmaster's office right now.

!

to hit the nail on the head
den Nagel auf den Kopf treffen

125 **A turtleneck sweater**

Mom, all the guys would laugh at me if I wore this.

What's wrong with it? It looks really nice on you.

Turtleneck sweaters just aren't cool.

Listen Charlie, it's a shame to let perfectly good clothes go to waste. Your other things are full of holes.

But that's the way I like them.

My son is not going to walk around like a bum.

Couldn't we go shopping and buy some new ones?

No, I have neither the time nor the patience to go shopping with you. Trying to find a sweater that we both approve of is like looking for a needle in a haystack.

126 **In the library**

You know the picture of the President that was hanging in front of his office? Someone's taken it.

Mason Devonport is amazing. He really keeps us all on our toes.

Yes, well, the headmaster can't prove that he's done it. He has all of the younger boys searching the dormitories and the grounds, trying to find it.

Poor boys. If Mason Devonport hid it, they've got their hands full. Remember when he stole the headmaster's jacket and we didn't find it until the next winter? Take my word for it, looking for something that Mason Devonport has hidden is like looking for a needle in a haystack.

like looking for a needle in a haystack

als ob man eine Nadel im Heuhaufen suchte

!

127 The chemistry teacher

Mom, if you force me to wear this sweater, you're going to ruin me socially. It looks like something Mr. Schultz would wear.

Mr. Schultz? Isn't he that nice man who teaches chemistry? I think he was teaching when your father went to school.

No, that was Davidson. Schultz teaches geography. Gee, Mom, you sure are out of touch. Davidson kicked the bucket last year. Remember, school was cancelled, so the teachers could go to the old geezer's funeral.

128 In the gymnasium

It appears someone covered the basketballs with glue and now this one is stuck to poor Arnold's hands.

Calm down, Arnold, we'll take you to Mr. Russell, the chemistry teacher. I'm sure he has something that will dissolve the glue.

Mason Devonport had his P.E. lesson this morning. The headmaster is giving him the third degree right now in his office.

I imagine the headmaster is really looking forward to the day Mason graduates and leaves Argyle.

Not true. Mason's pranks add a lot of excitement to the old fellow's day. Mason keeps him young and active. Believe me, if another smart aleck doesn't come along after Mason graduates, our dear old headmaster'll kick the bucket from all the boredom.

!

to kick the bucket
sterben; den Löffel aus der Hand legen
(den Eimer treten)

129 The family car

And it was about time too. The old guy was blind as a bat. Me and the guys always sat in the back and slept ...

Charles, I can't believe my ears! How dare you talk about one of your teachers like that! Your teachers work hard, and you should show them more respect. Wait till your father hears about the trouble you've been giving me. I don't think he'll be so anxious to give you the keys to the car ...

Oh, Mom, stop, stop. I'm really, truly sorry, believe me. No need to fly off the handle like that.

130 In the copy room

I'm sorry, but I don't know how to fix it. It looks like some of the parts are missing. I think we'll have to call the janitor.

That's just wonderful! What about the examination I was going to give the students today? They can't write an exam if they don't have the questions. When I get my hands on Mason Devonport, I'll ...

Calm down! Just write all the problems on the blackboard and make the pupils copy them onto a piece of paper. When dealing with Mason, it's better to stay calm than to fly off the handle.

to fly off the handle
die Fassung verlieren; fuchsteufelswild werden
(vom Griff wegfliegen)

!

131 An apology

I never should have said any of that stuff. I apologize.

So now you're sorry. What about the sweater? You're going to wear it to school tomorrow, aren't you?

Oh, Mom, that isn't fair ...

Walking is very good for your health, you know, I'm sure your father will agree ...

Stop. I must be out of my mind, but, yes, I'll wear it. Can I borrow the car on Friday night if I do?

I don't think that'll cause any problems.

Gee, you sure drive a hard bargain. My buddies are never going to let me hear the end of this. And the girls, oh the girls, are going to treat me like a leper. Peggy'll never go out with me now. My love life is going down the drain.

132 In the teachers' room

It's gone! The janitor's looked everywhere, but he can't find the missing part.

He doesn't have any spare parts in his office!? Is it so difficult to be prepared for repairs, especially when they're so simple? And who left the door to the copy room unlocked? It's sad to say, but this school is really going down the drain.

down the drain
den Bach runtergehen
(den Abfluss runter)

!

133 A teenage beauty

Heck, I guess I'm destined for a life of celibacy.
Oh, Charlie, get serious. Peggy who?
Peggy Bernelli, a work of art. Long auburn hair and the most incredible legs that ...
Watch it, young man. Remember this is your mother you're talking to.
Sorry, but she's really smart, too. Top of the class. I'd give anything to have her help me with my homework.
Well, I suppose a little tutoring couldn't hurt.
Yeah, well, she told Billy Tervelle that I was the cutest basketball player she'd ever seen. I was going to ask her to a movie on Friday and she would have said yes, I'm sure. I had her in the bag, but now this turtleneck ...

134 In the boys' dormitory

They actually caught him red-handed?
Yes, the headmaster and Mr. Thompson walked into his room while he was trying to stuff the missing part under his roommate's mattress. Mason can't deny that he stole it.
Well, it appears that the headmaster finally has Mason's suspension in the bag.

!

in the bag
unter Dach und Fach haben
(in der Tasche)

135 A football player

But now Peggy won't give me a second look.
Charlie, the sweater isn't that bad. This style is back in fashion now.
Yeah? Well, Greg Simmons doesn't have a sweater like this.
Who's Greg Simmons? The name sounds familiar.
He's the quarterback of the football team. Almost a god. All the girls worship him — except for Peggy Bernelli. But he sure wouldn't mind if she did.
Well, nobody can steal a girl away from my handsome son.
I thought so too, but when she lays eyes on this sweater, she's going to run right into Simmons' arms. I guess I should just let Simmons have her and save myself the humiliation. It's better to throw in the towel.

136 In the dining hall

Well, the headmaster isn't in a very good mood tonight. He's barely touched his food.
He arranged for a hearing, so he can suspend Mason, and the boy asked that his father be present.
His father? That Mason certainly is a fighter. Since his father graduated from Argyle, he's donated enormous sums of money to the school. It's going to be rather difficult for the headmaster to suspend Mason when his father's around. Mason hasn't thrown in the towel.

to throw in the towel/sponge
die Flinte ins Korn werfen; das Handtuch werfen
(das Handtuch/den Schwamm hinwerfen)

137

A nice girl

Guess I'll just become a monk. Looks like you'll have to adopt some grandchildren.

Sometimes I really wonder if there's a brain in your skull. Charlie, if Peggy Bernelli really likes you, she won't be worrying about your sweater when you ask her out. I don't remember what your father was wearing when he first asked me out.

Yeah, but that was twenty years ago. You just forgot.

Smart aleck. People nowadays are just too worried about what's on the surface. If Peggy is as wonderful as you think, she won't care what you wear, and you should behave the same way. You shouldn't judge a book by its cover.

138

In the parking lot

I was right. Mason's father got him off the hook. He marched into the headmaster's office and put his foot down. He threatened to cut off all his donations. The headmaster really wants a new gymnasium, so he had to give in.

Mason got off scot-free?

No, he has to clean the school grounds every day after his lessons.

His father must be a real monster to intimidate our headmaster ...

There he is. Over there by the big Mercedes.

That little fellow with the big ears and the bald head? He looks like he couldn't hurt a fly.

Well, don't judge a book by its cover.

!

not to judge a book by its cover

nicht aufgrund von Äußerlichkeiten urteilen, der Schein könnte trügen

(ein Buch nicht nach seinem Umschlag bewerten)

139 Charlie the Courageous

You sure do know how to put on the pressure. Looks like I don't have much of a choice. I'll wear the sweater. Can I turn the TV on now? The movie's going to start.

Okay, I get the hint. I'll clear out of here, and you can watch your movie.

Thanks.

Thank you, Charlie. It's good to know that my boy has got guts.

Aw, Mom, knock it off. Don't make such a big deal about it. Heck, I'm no wimp. Sometimes you just have to stop whining and bite the bullet.

140 Behind the boys' dormitory

Is that the headmaster out there with Mason Devonport?

Yes, it is.

What are they doing out there?

The headmaster is personally supervising Mason's work. Every afternoon he stands and watches the boy work. Yesterday he made him trim the grass around the trees with a scissors.

Poor Mason, that must be torture.

Well, he doesn't have any other choice. Until the headmaster calms down, he'll just have to bite the bullet.

to bite the bullet
die Zähne zusammenbeißen; etwas durchstehen; tapfer sein (die Kugel beißen)

!

121 Charlie's mother

deaf
taub

to pretend
vortäuschen

to wrestle
ringen

to pick up a bad habit
eine schlechte Angewohnheit/Unart annehmen

122 At the Argyle School for Young Men

headmaster
Schulleiter

obnoxious
nervig; abscheulich

rascal
Strolch

to disrupt
stören; unterbrechen

to get into mischief
etwas «anstellen»

123 A box of old clothes

dying to
kaum erwarten können

to get down to business
eine Sache in Angriff nehmen

to try something on
etwas anprobieren

Salvation Army
Heilsarmee

rag
Lumpen

124 In the dining hall

salt shaker
Salzstreuer

staff
Personal; Belegschaft

to unscrew
losschrauben

lid
Deckel

to sprinkle
streuen

mashed potatoes
Kartoffelbrei

to get more than one bargained for
mehr als erwartet bekommen

prank
Streich

125 A turtleneck sweater

turtleneck sweater
Rollkragenpullover

to let something go to waste
etwas kaputtgehen lassen; etwas vergeuden

bum
Gammler

to approve of
akzeptieren; billigen

126 In the library

to keep someone on his/her toes
jemanden in Trab halten

dormitory
Schlafsäle

to have one's hands full
alle Hände voll zu tun haben

to take someone's word for it
jemandes Worten Glauben schenken

127 The chemistry teacher

out of touch
den Anschluss verpasst haben

old geezer
alter Knacker

funeral
Beerdigung

128 In the gymnasium

gymnasium
Turnhalle

to be stuck to
festsitzen an

to dissolve
auflösen

P.E.
physical education = Sportunterricht

to give someone the third degree
jemanden ins Kreuzverhör nehmen

to graduate
einen Schul- oder Universitätsabschluss machen

smart aleck
Klugscheißer

boredom
Langeweile

129 The family car

blind as a bat
blind wie eine Fledermaus

130 In the copy room

janitor
Hausmeister

to get one's hands on ...
... in die Finger kriegen

problems
hier: Aufgaben

131 An apology

to drive a hard bargain
mit harten Bandagen kämpfen; knallhart verhandeln

buddy
Kumpel

not to let someone hear the end of this
jemandem keine Ruhe mehr geben; etwas immer wieder erwähnen; immer wieder an einer Sache rühren

to treat someone like a leper
jemanden wie einen Aussätzigen behandeln

132 In the teachers' room

spare parts
Ersatzteile

133 A teenage beauty

life of celibacy
zölibatäres, enthaltsames Leben

to be top of the class
Klassenbester sein

to tutor someone
jemandem Nachhilfeunterricht geben

cute
hübsch; gut aussehend

134 In the boys' dormitory

to catch someone red-handed
jemanden auf frischer Tat ertappen

to deny
leugnen

suspension
Schulausschluss

135 A football player

not to give someone a second look
jemanden keines zweiten Blickes würdigen

quarterback
wichtigster Spieler im amerikanischen Football

to worship
verehren

to lay eyes on ...
... betrachten

to save oneself the humiliation
sich die Demütigung ersparen

136 In the dining hall

hearing
Anhörung

to donate
spenden

137 A nice girl

monk
Mönch

skull
Schädel

surface
Oberfläche

138 In the parking lot

to get someone off the hook
jemanden loseisen; jemanden retten

to put one's foot down
einen festen Standpunkt einnehmen; seine Meinung klar machen

donation
Spende

to give in
nachgeben

to get off scot-free
ungestraft davonkommen

to intimidate
einschüchtern

He couldn't hurt a fly.
Er könnte keiner Fliege etwas zuleide tun.

139 Charlie the Courageous

to put on the pressure
unter Druck setzen

to get the hint
den zarten Hinweis (eine Anspielung, indirekte Aufforderung) verstehen

to clear out of here
sich dünnmachen

to have guts
Mut haben; wörtlich: Därme haben

to knock it off
ein Thema beenden

to make a big deal about ...
ein Riesentheater wegen ... machen

heck
Euphemismus für «hell»; Mensch!

wimp
Waschlappen; Schlappschwanz

to whine
rumjammern

140 Behind the boys' dormitory

to trim grass
Rasenkanten trimmen

scissors
Schere

torture
Qual

1. What's the best answer?

1. You can't give up now. Don't
- **a** bite the bullet!
- **b** throw in the towel!
- **c** kick the bucket!

2. I know Mary wears thick glasses and she isn't very pretty, but she still might be very nice. You shouldn't
- **a** fly off the handle.
- **b** judge a book by its cover.
- **c** hit the nail on the head.

3. I've convinced him you're the best candidate. His support is
- **a** in the bag.
- **b** going down the drain.
- **c** a chip off the old block.

4. We'll never find it! This is like
- **a** looking for a needle in a haystack.
- **b** looking for a chip off the old block.
- **c** hitting the nail on the head.

5. You're exactly right! You've
- **a** kicked the bucket.
- **b** bitten the bullet.
- **c** hit the nail on the head.

6. Ever since he lied to me, our friendship has been
- **a** in the bag.
- **b** a chip off the old block.
- **c** going down the drain.

2. Say it using an idiom

1. Don't cry. You have to accept this as bravely as possible.

2. He's just like his father.

3. When you tell her, she'll probably become very angry.

4. Ben knew he couldn't win, so he gave up.

5. That old dog finally died.

6. You were exactly right when you said George was a thief.

7. Trying to find your contact lens is a very difficult thing to do.

8. We're going to win the game. It is certain we'll win.

9. Our plans to have a picnic were spoiled when it started to rain.

10. You shouldn't judge a person by his appearance.

3. Match the phrases

1. Stop complaining! I know it won't be easy, but sometimes you just have to...
2. Maybe you should listen to me before you get angry. You always...
3. Our teachers are poorly paid and the schools don't have money for new books and computers. Our educational system is going...
4. I need my inheritance now. I wish my father would...
5. This may look like a piece of rubbish, but it's actually very valuable. You shouldn't...
6. You think you'll find Julia in this crowd? I'd rather look...
7. I know Whitney'll go to the dance with you. Believe me, you have her...
8. Michael Douglas is just like his father. He's...
9. We'll never finish this by the deadline. We'll have to...
10. When Descartes said «I think, therefore I am,» he...

- **a.** ...kick the bucket.
- **b.** ...throw in the towel.
- **c.** ...down the drain.
- **d.** ...for a needle in a haystack.
- **e.** ...bite the bullet.
- **f.** ...fly off the handle.
- **g.** ...in the bag.
- **h.** ...hit the nail on the head.
- **i.** ...judge a book by its cover.
- **j.** ...a chip off the old block.

Answers: 1. ☐ 2. ☐ 3. ☐ 4. ☐ 5. ☐ 6. ☐ 7. ☐ 8. ☐ 9. ☐ 10. ☐

4. Translate

1. Alles geht den Bach runter.

....

....

2. Du wirst es nie finden, du suchst eine Nadel im Heuhaufen.

....

....

3. Er hat die Fassung verloren.

....

....

4. Du solltest die Flinte nicht ins Korn werfen.

....

....

5. Dein Sohn ist ganz der Vater.

....

....

6. Du hast es unter Dach und Fach.

....

....

7. Sei tapfer!

....

....

8. Er ist endlich gestorben.

....

....

9. Aufpassen! Der Schein könnte trügen.

....

....

10. Du hast den Nagel auf den Kopf getroffen.

....

....

TOPIC 8

ODDS & ENDS

141 In a restaurant

Oh Dolly dear, you're a sight for sore eyes.
Morning, Tom! What can I get for you today? The usual?
Here, a present for you. How about a kiss?
A rose? Oh, it's beautiful. You're so sweet. Thanks. — A lot of hungry customers are waiting for their breakfasts. You'd better hurry and order or you'll be late for work.
I've got the day off. I'm just going to sit here all day on this stool and watch you.
What's going on? First a flower, and now your company for the whole day. This isn't like you. What other surprises do you have up your sleeve?

142 George and Fred

Hello, George. Come in. You're right on time!
Hi, Fred. I came right over after work. Your message said it was urgent.
You remember that new kung fu film I was telling you about?
Of course. I tried to get a copy of it at the video store, but it was checked out.
Well, I've got a surprise for you. I'm the one who checked it out, and we're going to watch it tonight.
I don't believe it. This is fantastic.
That's not all. I've got some beer in the fridge, there's a frozen pizza ...
Fred, you're great. You never cease to amaze me, seems like you've always got something up your sleeve.

!

up one's sleeve
etwas in petto haben; etwas auf Lager haben (in jemandes Ärmel)

143 The pet store

Well, Dolly, how about that kiss?
Stop it, Tom, or I'll drop your breakfast in your lap.
Mmmm, smells good. What would I do without you?
Flirt with some other waitress, I imagine. Now let's be serious for a minute. How come you're not going to work today?
Steve's there. He'll take care of everything. I just needed to get away from that stupid pet store.
But you love the pet store. You aren't sick, are you?
No, but lately I've had to force myself to go to work and take care of those animals. I don't really enjoy it anymore. I've just been going through the motions.

144 Cleaning up

George, when I let you move in with me, we made some agreements, remember?
Yeah, Fred, I pay half of the rent.
And you do half of the work around here.
Listen, an hour ago you told me to get off the couch and clean up the living room. So now I'm cleaning!
You call that cleaning? You're only pushing the vacuum cleaner around in circles. You have to move the furniture, so you can reach all the dust and dirt that's under there. You're just going through the motions. Stop wasting time and do it right.

!

to go through the motions
so tun, als ob; etwas völlig lustlos betreiben
(durch die Bewegungen gehen)

145 **Wedding bells**

It all started when Steve told me he was going to get married.

He is? Why didn't you tell me earlier? Who's the lucky girl?

A nice girl whose father owns a pencil factory.

So what's wrong with you? You should be happy for him.

Well, Steve's in seventh heaven. All he wants to talk about is the wedding and the honeymoon. That made me start thinking about marriage myself. It might be nice to have someone to talk to at the dinner table. Heck, I guess all that talk about marriage just rubbed off on me.

146 **Improvement**

I never thought I'd be saying this, but I can't deny it. George, this place looks great. It's spick and span. You did a great job of cleaning up around here.

Well, we don't want to live in a dump. What would the women we bring home think? Besides, cleaning is rather relaxing, like meditation. It's taken me a few weeks to learn, but I guess your good example has finally rubbed off on me.

!

to rub off on someone
auf jemanden abfärben
(auf jemanden abreiben)

147 A new face

Can you believe it? I've finally started thinking about getting married.
I think it's great, Tom. It's about time you get out and meet new people.
Well, there will be one new face in my store soon.
I don't follow you.
Steve's future father-in-law wants him to take over his company, so Steve is going to quit. It's going to be difficult to find a replacement who's half as good as Steve. As far as I'm concerned, his wedding is a mixed blessing.

148 Uncomfortable

George, I'm starting to have second thoughts.
About what, Fred?
About us sharing this apartment.
You are? Why? I've always paid the rent on time, and I've even learned to like cleaning.
Yeah, it's great having the extra money, and I appreciate all the work you do. It's these women you're bringing home all the time. I always have to tiptoe around when you've got them in your bedroom ... it's getting on my nerves. Sharing an apartment with you has turned out to be a mixed blessing.

!

a mixed blessing
ein zweischneidiges Schwert; eine zweischneidige Sache (ein gemischter Segen)

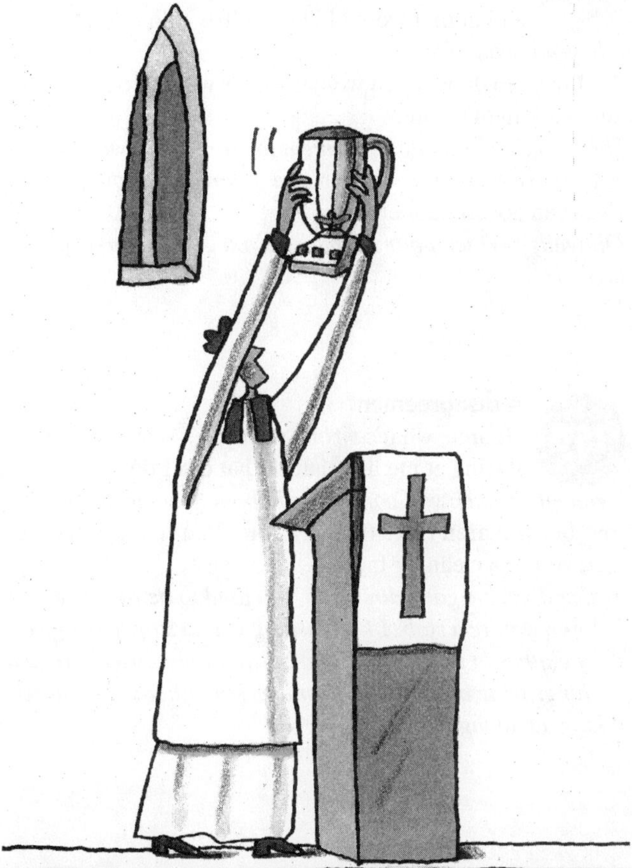

149

A solution

You know, Dolly, I was thinking and I came up with a plan that would kill two birds with one stone.

Oh, yeah, what plan?

All I have to do is find a woman who's willing to marry me and work in my store.

Now, wouldn't that be convenient for you? Poor woman. She'd have to put up with you and a store full of puppies.

I've even got someone in mind.

Oh really? Which poor woman are you going to take advantage of?

You.

150

A disagreement

George, what's wrong with you? Why are you staring at me like that? What did I do wrong?

Remember when you complained about how messy I was?

Yes, but you aren't like that anymore. You're reformed. In fact, you're a cleaning fanatic.

Yes, and you've gone downhill. You used to be really neat, but now you're a slob. I keep asking you to stop leaving your dirty clothes in the living room, but you don't listen. You leave things lying around and let me pick up after you. You're taking advantage of me!

!

to take advantage of someone
jemanden übervorteilen/ausnutzen
(von jemandem den Vorteil nehmen)

151

A problem

Well, Dolly, what do you say?

Oh my God, oh my God, oh my God. I should have known something like this would happen. I'll never forgive myself for letting things get out of hand.

Dolly, what's the matter?

Oh, Tom, you just wouldn't understand.

Whatever it is, tell me. I don't care. Are you married, seeing somebody? Maybe you've got three kids? None of that matters. We can work it out. All I want is for you to marry me. I don't give a damn about anything else.

152

Dr. Jekyll ...

You are really getting on my nerves, George. You're worse than my mother, complaining all the time. I left home, so I wouldn't have to listen to any of that anymore.

All of my complaints are valid, Fred. All of a sudden, you're lazy and you're no fun to be around anymore. What happened to the fun-loving guy I knew in college? I just want you to help me more with the housework, and I'd like to go out once in a while and have some fun.

Listen, George, we aren't married. This is my apartment, remember? I'm the one who signed the lease. I'm the guy in charge, and I don't give a damn about what you want.

not to give a damn
sich einen Dreck drum scheren
(keinen Fluch geben)

!

153

A surprise

Dolly, put the coffeepot down. You're shaking. Sit down by me and get if off your chest. Give me your hand.

God, Tom, I just don't know how to tell you this.

Don't beat around the bush, just say it.

Okay. Man, this isn't easy. — Tom, I ... I'm a transvestite.

Is that all? That's nothing to worry ... Wait a minute! You're a transvestite!? You mean, you're a man with a penis and stuff like that?

Yes, Tom.

No way, this can't be happening to me. I'm sitting next to a man. Ugh, get up, get out of here, and get your hands off me. Don't touch me! You give me the creeps.

154

... and Mr. Hyde

What's wrong now?

That's what I want to know, Fred. You're on vacation, you're supposed to have a good time. Instead you're sitting in the living room with the curtains closed, watching horror movies. I'm getting worried. When was the last time you took a shower or brushed your teeth? The way you're behaving is giving me the creeps.

!

to give someone the creeps

jemandem ein unbehagliches Schauern/Gruseln/
eine Gänsehaut verursachen
(jemandem das Gruseln geben)

155 Friends again

Since you were fifteen? And I never noticed.
I didn't come out of the closet until I turned 20. You're taking this very well.
Well, I'm always telling people to be more liberal, so I guess I should practice what I preach. Wait till Steve hears I proposed to a guy named Douglas. You really fooled me.
Amazing what a wig and some falsies can do, huh?
This is kind of weird, but I've got a favor to ask.
What?
I'd like to see what you really look like. I mean, it's not that important, not a matter of life and death. Just for the hell of it.

156 A confession

No George, I'm not on vacation. I was fired and my girlfriend broke up with me.
God, Fred, is that all? I thought you were really nuts.
Well, I'm glad you're relieved.
Cheer up! You'll get a new job, and there are plenty of women who'd love to date a guy like you. Let's go out tonight and look for some company.
No, I don't feel like getting involved in another relationship. I really loved that girl.
Okay, no hurry. You don't have to start looking tonight. Let's just go out for a beer. Just for the hell of it.

just for the hell of it
nur zum Spaß; aus Jux und Tollerei
(nur für die Hölle davon)

!

157 Douglas

So this is what it looks like inside the Ladies' Room. Dirtier than I imagined. Hey, are you almost ready?
Ready. Close your eyes and don't open them till I count to three. One, two, three. Ta-dah!
You're quite handsome, Douglas.
Still want to marry me?
Stop it! I'm looking for a member of the opposite sex.
Okay, I get the picture. Well, next time wait till she's taken off her clothes before you ask. That way you won't be disappointed again.
Yeah, it's better to be safe than sorry.

158 A new start

Thanks for dragging me out of that apartment, George. I feel much better.
All you needed was a change of scenery, Fred.
Yeah, have you noticed that girl on the other side of the bar? She's checking you out, George.
Not me, y-o-u! Why don't you go over there and offer to buy her a drink?
No, I can't just leave you here by yourself.
Yes, you can. I don't mind. Good luck! But remember, always wear a condom. Better safe than sorry.

!

better safe than sorry
lieber auf Nummer Sicher gehen
(besser sicher als bedauernd)

Curiosity

159 This wig sure does look like real hair, Doug.
It should. Cost me an arm and a leg.
I wonder what I'd look like with a wig like that on.
You'll never know if you don't try. Put it on.
No, I couldn't do that. Somebody might see me.
I locked the door. Go ahead. Tony Curtis did it in «Some like it hot», and so did Dustin Hoffman in «Tootsie».
You're sure you wouldn't mind?
Not at all. Go ahead, Tom. Be my guest.

A new love

160 Hey, George, I'd like you to meet Sheila Weston. Sheila, this is George, my best friend.
Nice to meet you, Sheila. Are you two leaving so soon?
Yes, Sheila's got a great collection of kung fu films at her place, so we're going over there. Want to come?
No, thanks. Three's a crowd.
Uh, George, remember what you were saying before, about being safe? Well, I didn't bring anything like that with me. I probably won't need it, but you never know.
No problem, Fred. There's a box in the glove compartment of my car. Be my guest.

Be my guest.
Bedien dich; nimm dir, was du brauchst.
(Sei mein Gast.)

!

141 In a restaurant

a sight for sore eyes
ein willkommener Anblick

The usual?
Das Übliche?

stool
Hocker

What's going on?
Was geht denn hier vor?

This isn't like you.
Das sieht dir aber überhaupt nicht ähnlich.

142 George and Fred

to check something out
etwas ausleihen

to cease
aufhören

143 The pet store

lap
Schoß

how come
wieso

144 Cleaning up

to move in with someone
zu jemandem in die Wohnung ziehen

145 Wedding bells

Who's the lucky girl?
Wer ist denn die Glückliche?

to be happy for him
sich mit ihm freuen

to be in seventh heaven
im siebten Himmel sein

honeymoon
Flitterwochen

146 Improvement

spick (auch: spic) and span
blitzblank

dump
Dreckloch

147 A new face

I don't follow you.
Ich kann dir nicht ganz folgen.

future father-in-law
zukünftiger Schwiegervater

to be half as good as
auch nur halb so gut sein wie

148 Uncomfortable

to have second thoughts
Zweifel bekommen; es sich doch noch anders überlegen

to share an apartment
zusammen wohnen

to tiptoe
auf Zehenspitzen gehen

149 A solution

to kill two birds with one stone
siehe «Animal Kingdom» 1/2

puppy
Hündchen

to have someone in mind
schon wissen, wer

150 A disagreement

to stare at
anstarren

messy
unordentlich; schlampig

to go downhill
immer weiter bergab gehen

neat
ordentlich

slob
Schlamper

to pick up after someone
jemandes Dreck wegmachen

151 A problem

to get out of hand
außer Kontrolle geraten

to see somebody
mit jemandem regelmäßig ausgehen

to work something out
eine Lösung finden

152 Dr. Jekyll ...

valid
gültig; berechtigt

all of a sudden
plötzlich

You're no fun to be around.
Es macht keinen Spaß, mit dir zusammen zu sein.

lease
Mietvertrag

to be in charge
verantwortlich sein

153 A surprise

Get it if off your chest.
Erleichtere dein Herz; spuck's aus.

to beat around the bush
siehe «Nature» 93/94

154 ... and Mr. Hyde

to have a good time
sich amüsieren

155 Friends again

to come out of the closet
sich «outen»; sich öffentlich zu etwas bekennen

to take something well
etwas gut aufnehmen

to practice what one preaches
nicht nur Sprüche klopfen, sondern auch entsprechend handeln

to propose to someone
jemandem einen Heiratsantrag machen

falsies
Schaumstoffbusen

weird
freakig; unheimlich; seltsam

to ask a favor
um einen Gefallen bitten

It's a matter of life and death.
Es geht um Leben oder Tod.

156 A confession

confession
Geständnis; Beichte

to be nuts
verrückt sein

to be relieved
erleichtert sein

157 Douglas

Ladies' Room
Damentoilette

Ta-dah!
Ausruf, der lautmalerisch einen Tusch imitiert

opposite sex
das andere Geschlecht

158 A new start

to drag
zerren

a change of scenery
Tapetenwechsel

159 Curiosity

to cost an arm and a leg
ein Heidengeld kosten

Go ahead!
Mach doch, los geht's!

Three's a crowd.
Drei sind einer zu viel.

glove compartment
Handschuhfach

TOPIC 8 EXERCISES

1. What's the best answer?

1. He doesn't really like doing his job. He's just
- **a** going through the motions.
- **b** taking of advantage of it.
- **c** keeping something up his sleeve.

2. If you want to try my computer,
- **a** better safe than sorry.
- **b** be my guest.
- **c** it'll rub off on you.

3. You are always full of surprises. What other tricks do you
- **a** go through the motions?
- **b** not give a damn about?
- **c** have up your sleeve?

4. We encourage our son to play with Molly. We hope her good behavior will
- **a** give him the creeps.
- **b** be a mixed blessing.
- **c** rub off on him.

5. I had no special reason for doing that. I did it
- **a** because it's better to be safe than sorry.
- **b** just for the hell of it.
- **c** to take advantage of you.

6. I don't like sitting next to him, because
- **a** he gives me the creeps.
- **b** he might rub off on me.
- **c** he's my guest.

2. Say it using an idiom

1. You made unfair use of my kindness.

2. A baby is something good, but it also has some disadvantages.

3. I'm sure he has a plan he's keeping secret until we really need it.

4. Some more coffee? Feel free to help yourself.

5. It's better to prepare yourself, so that you can avoid disappointment.

6. Rhett Butler told Scarlett that he didn't care anymore.

7. Arnold hit him for no particular reason, just for fun.

8. Janet was doing it without really caring or enjoying it.

9. You're so intelligent. If we study together, some of your intelligence might influence me.

10. Snakes make me feel very frightened and disgusted.

3. Match the phrases

1. I'm sure he has some information we don't know about…
2. Come on, you have to work harder. Right now you're only…
3. He won the lottery again?! I wish some of his luck would…
4. That cat makes the kids happy, but it's always peeing on the furniture. It's really…
5. He doesn't really like you, he just wants your money. He is just…
6. I want that car and I don't…
7. Let's get out of this empty building. It's so dark in here. It really…
8. Why do I want to take you out to dinner? No special reason,…
9. Always wear a condom,…
10. Go ahead, have a second piece of cake,…

a. …going through the motions.
b. …a mixed blessing.
c. …give a damn how much it costs.
d. …just for the hell of it.
e. …better safe than sorry.
f. …be my guest.
g. …gives me the creeps.
h. …taking advantage of you.
i. …rub off on me.
j. …up his sleeve.

Answers: 1. ☐ 2. ☐ 3. ☐ 4. ☐ 5. ☐ 6. ☐ 7. ☐ 8. ☐ 9. ☐ 10. ☐

4. Translate

1. Das ist ein zweischneidiges Schwert.

....

....

2. Ich wette, sie hat noch etwas auf Lager.

....

....

3. Ich kriege das Gruseln, wenn ich ihn sehe.

....

....

4. Sie schert sich einen Dreck drum.

....

....

5. Ich gebe dir einen Rat: lieber auf Nummer Sicher gehen.

....

....

6. Sex macht Alexis keinen Spaß, sie tut nur so, als ob.

....

....

7. Bedien dich!

....

....

8. Sie will mich ausnutzen.

....

....

9. Er tut das nur aus Jux und Tollerei.

....

....

10. Vielleicht wird dein Glück auf mich abfärben.

....

....

ANSWERS

1

1. What's the best answer? 1. c - **2.** b - **3.** a - **4.** a - **5.** c - **6.** b

2. Say it using an idiom: 1. Don't tell your grandmother. Let sleeping dogs lie. **2.** Your bark is worse than your bite. **3.** Don't listen to him, he's always crying wolf. **4.** You can't teach an old dog new tricks. **5.** I got this information straight from the horse's mouth. **6.** I didn't do anything when you said I was rude and stupid, but when you called me a thief, that was the straw that broke the camel's back. **7.** When you said he was too fat, you ruffled his feathers. **8.** Just take the bull by the horns! **9.** I want to put this motorcycle through its paces before I buy it. **10.** That will kill two birds with one stone.

3. Match the phrases: 1. e - **2.** i - **3.** a - **4.** c - **5.** b - **6.** h - **7.** j - **8.** g - **9.** f - **10.** d

4. Translate: 1. Don't be afraid. His bark is worse than his bite. **2.** Don't worry! The boy is only crying wolf. **3.** Don't waste any time! Take the bull by the horns! **4.** You can't teach old dogs new tricks! **5.** This way we can kill two birds with one stone. **6.** Before we hire Mr. Schmidt, I'd like to put him through his paces. **7.** I heard/got that straight from the horse's mouth. **8.** You really ruffled her feathers. **9.** Let sleeping dogs lie. **10.** That is the straw that broke the camel's back.

2

1. What's the best answer? 1. c - **2.** a - **3.** c - **4.** c - **5.** a - **6.** b

2. Say it using an idiom: 1. You know that I was fired!? Who spilled the beans? **2.** If you butter him up, he might let you drive his new car. **3.** You can't eat your cake and have it too. **4.** Babysitting is his cup of tea. **5.** This teacher is the cream of the crop. **6.** Now that I don't live with my parents anymore, I have to bring home the bacon. **7.** Learning English is a piece of cake. **8.** I will make you eat your words. **9.** Don't cry over spilled milk. **10.** He bit off more than he can chew.

3. Match the phrases: 1. g - **2.** a - **3.** d - **4.** j - **5.** h - **6.** b - **7.** e - **8.** f - **9.** i - **10.** c

4. Translate: 1. Don't cry over spilled milk. **2.** Who spilled the beans? **3.** He had to eat his words. **4.** It's a piece of cake. **5.** That isn't my cup of tea. **6.** You can't eat your cake and have it too. **7.** How can we butter him up? **8.** I think I bit off more than I can chew. **9.** This man is the cream of the crop. **10.** Who brings home the bacon in your family?

3

1. What's the best answer? 1. b - **2.** c - **3.** b - **4.** a - **5.** b - **6.** c

2. Say it using an idiom: 1. You took the words right out of my mouth. **2.** Stop crying! Keep a stiff upper lip! **3.** The sight of blood turns my stomach. **4.** I'll never knuckle under. **5.** I'm only pulling your leg. **6.** I hope I'll win the race. Keep your fingers crossed. **7.** I'm head over heels in love with her.
8. When I lived in Hollywood, I often rubbed elbows/shoulders with famous actors at parties. **9.** My little sister is a pain in the neck/ass. **10.** He looks down his nose at me, because I didn't study at Harvard.

3. Match the phrases: 1. f - **2.** j - **3.** a - **4.** d - **5.** b - **6.** i - **7.** g - **8.** c - **9.** e - **10.** h

4. Translate: 1. Raw meat turns my stomach. **2.** Keep a stiff upper lip! **3.** You took the words right out of my mouth. **4.** He will eventually knuckle under. **5.** My wife is a real pain in the neck/ass. **6.** In London I rubbed elbows/shoulders with very important people. **7.** You shouldn't look down your nose at him. **8.** She is head over heels in love with him. **9.** Are you pulling my leg? **10.** Keep your fingers crossed.

4

1. What's the best answer? 1. a - **2.** a - **3.** b - **4.** b - **5.** c - **6.** c

2. Say it using an idiom: 1. Don't sell him short! He can do it! **2.** I have to find him. Money is no object. **3.** We are finding it very difficult to make ends meet. **4.** He should mind his own business. **5.** You said you'd buy me a new dress, so now you'd better put your money where your mouth is.
6. Frank doesn't have a penny to his name. **7.** I think Alice is sold on spending a week in the Caribbean. **8.** When the dog started barking, he ran for all he was worth. **9.** Don't go. I'm certain we can strike a bargain. **10.** You hit the jackpot when you married that girl. She's perfect.

3. Match the phrases: 1. b - **2.** j - **3.** e - **4.** i - **5.** a - **6.** d - **7.** f - **8.** h - **9.** c - **10.** g

4. Translate: 1. I don't have a penny to my name. **2.** I fought back for all I was worth. **3.** Somehow we'll strike a bargain. **4.** I am sold on that plan. **5.** Believe me, money is no object. **6.** We can't make ends meet. **7.** We should mind our own business. **8.** We sold him short. **9.** You should put your money where your mouth is. **10.** I hit the jackpot.

5

1. What's the best answer? 1. c - **2.** a - **3.** b - **4.** b - **5.** a - **6.** c

2. Say it using an idiom: 1. The police will leave no stone unturned to find the missing child. **2.** Whenever I ask him, he beats around/about the bush. **3.** How did you get wind of my plans? **4.** My mother is a stick-in-the-mud. **5.** It never rains but it pours. **6.** Come hell or high water, I will always love you. **7.** We are up the creek (without a paddle). **8.** This is only the tip of the iceberg. **9.** Young men want to sow their wild oats before they get married. **10.** We have to nip this drug problem in the bud.

3. Match the phrases: 1. j - **2.** i - **3.** b - **4.** d - **5.** f - **6.** h - **7.** e - **8.** g - **9.** c - **10.** a

4. Translate: 1. It never rains but it pours. **2.** You have to nip the problem in the bud. **3.** She really makes me angry. She's always beating around the bush. **4.** How did he get wind of it? **5.** My husband is a stick-in-the-mud. **6.** Bernie has to sow his wild oats. **7.** We will leave no stone unturned. **8.** You'll do it, come hell or high water. **9.** He's up the creek (without a paddle). **10.** This is only the tip of the iceberg.

6

1. What's the best answer? 1. c - **2.** b - **3.** a - **4.** c - **5.** b - **6.** a

2. Say it using an idiom: 1. I'm sure she'll find something to do to kill time. **2.** Now that exams are right around the corner, a lot of students are burning the midnight oil. **3.** You spoke too soon. **4.** I will get into an airplane when hell freezes over. **5.** Your phone call made my day. **6.** Today is not my day. **7.** Richard get married? That'll be the day. **8.** Time flies when you're having fun. **9.** You want me to do my homework? All in good time. **10.** He jumped from in front of the train in the nick of time.

3. Match the phrases: **1.** f - **2.** h - **3.** d - **4.** g - **5.** b - **6.** j - **7.** e - **8.** i - **9.** c - **10.** a

4. Translate: **1.** This gift/present made my day. **2.** You spoke too soon. **3.** You came in the nick of time. **4.** That'll be the day. **5.** I'll kiss you when hell freezes over. **6.** Time flies when you're having fun. **7.** If I want to finish this, I'll have to burn the midnight oil. **8.** Today is not my day. **9.** How can we kill time? **10.** All in good time.

7

1. What's the best answer? **1.** b - **2.** b - **3.** a - **4.** a - **5.** c - **6.** c

2. Say it using an idiom: **1.** Don't cry! You have to bite the bullet. **2.** He's a chip off the old block. **3.** When you tell her, she'll probably fly off the handle. **4.** Ben knew he couldn't win, so he threw in the towel/sponge. **5.** That old dog finally kicked the bucket. **6.** You hit the nail on the head when you said George was a thief. **7.** Trying to find your contact lens is like looking for a needle in a haystack.
8. We've got the game in the bag. **9.** Our plans to have a picnic went down the drain when it started to rain. **10.** You shouldn't judge a book by its cover.

3. Match the phrases: **1.** e - **2.** f - **3.** c - **4.** a - **5.** i - **6.** d - **7.** g - **8.** j - **9.** b - **10.** h

4. Translate: 1. Everything's going down the drain. **2.** You'll never find it, you're looking for a needle in a haystack. **3.** He flew off the handle. **4.** You shouldn't throw in the towel/ sponge. **5.** Your son is a chip off the old block. **6.** You have it in the bag. **7.** Bite the bullet! **8.** He finally kicked the bucket. **9.** Be careful! Don't judge a book by its cover. **10.** You hit the nail on the head.

8

1. What's the best answer? 1. a - **2.** b - **3.** c - **4.** c - **5.** b - **6.** a

2. Say it using an idiom: 1. You took advantage of my kindness. **2.** A baby is a mixed blessing. **3.** I'm sure he has a plan up his sleeve. **4.** Some more coffee? Be my guest. **5.** Better safe than sorry./It's better to be safe than sorry. **6.** Rhett Butler told Scarlett that he didn't give a damn. **7.** Arnold hit him just for the hell of it. **8.** Janet was only going through the motions. **9.** You're so intelligent. If we study together, your intelligence might rub off on me. **10.** Snakes give me the creeps.

3. Match the phrases: 1. j - **2.** a - **3.** i - **4.** b - **5.** h - **6.** c - **7.** g - **8.** d - **9.** e - **10.** f

4. Translate: 1. That's a mixed blessing. **2.** I bet she has something up her sleeve. **3.** He gives me the creeps. **4.** She doesn't give a damn. **5.** I'll give you some advice: better safe than sorry. **6.** Alexis doesn't enjoy sex, she just goes through the motions. **7.** Be my guest! **8.** She wants to take advantage of me. **9.** He's doing it just for the hell of it. **10.** Maybe your luck will rub off on me.

Dieser Überblick über rund tausend geläufige idiomatische Redewendungen und Redensarten ist, was niemanden überraschen wird, alphabetisch angeordnet. Als Stichwort fungiert meist das erste Hauptwort des jeweiligen Ausdrucks, beispielsweise «nail: to hit the nail on the head». Gibt es kein Hauptwort, wird der gesamte Ausdruck unter dem Verb geführt, zum Beispiel «bend: to bend over backwards». Fehlt auch ein Verb, wird das für die Bedeutung wichtigste Wort als Stichwort angegeben.
Gelegentlich haben wir einen Beispielsatz gebildet, wenn die Bedeutung aus der unflektierten Form nicht klar hervorgeht. Feststehende Ausdrücke, die sich nicht konjugieren lassen, sind mit [*] gekennzeichnet.
Lediglich als Abkürzung erscheinen die Wörter «jemanden/jemandem/jemandes»: (jn., jm., js.).
Die Ziffer am Ende mancher Einträge verweist auf die Nummer der Szene, in der die jeweilige Wendung vorkommt, und nicht auf die Seitenzahl.

Einen Anspruch auf Vollständigkeit kann die folgende Liste in Anbetracht des idiomatischen Reichtums der englischen Sprache kaum erheben. Als weiterführende Literatur für den ambitionierten Lerner empfehlen sich die folgenden rein englischsprachigen Nachschlagewerke, die relativ häufig neu aufgelegt werden:

Robert James Dixson. *Essential Idioms in English.* Regents/Prentice Hall, 1994.

Adam Makkai, Maxine Tull Boatner, John E. Gates. *Dictionary of American Idioms.* 3rd Edition. Barrons Educational Series, 1995.

Richard A. Spears. *Ntc's American Idioms Dictionary. The Most Practical Reference for the Everyday Expressions of Contemporary American English.* National Textbook Co., 2000.

absence
Absence makes the heart grow fonder. [*] *Mit der Entfernung wächst die Sehnsucht.*

act
to act up *loslegen; Schwierigkeiten machen* **85**
to catch someone in the act *jn. auf frischer Tat ertappen*
to get one's act together *in Gang kommen; etwas auf die richtige Bahn bringen*

advantage
to take advantage of someone *jn. übervorteilen/ausnutzen* **149/150**
The advantages outweigh the disadvantages. *Die Vorteile überwiegen die Nachteile.* **56**

alive
to be eaten alive *bei lebendigem Leibe gefressen werden* **14/105**

almost
Almost there! [*] *Gleich haben wir's!* **116**

answer
to give a straight answer *ohne Umschweife antworten* **94**

appetite
to whet one's appetite for something *auf den Geschmack kommen; js. Appetit auf etwas wecken*

arm
to cost an arm and a leg *ein Heidengeld kosten* **67/159**
to keep at arm's length *auf Abstand halten*
to twist someone's arm *jn. zwingen*
to welcome someone with open arms *jn. mit offenen Armen willkommen heißen* **49**

ass
pompous ass *arroganter Arsch; aufgeblasener Kerl*

axe/ax
to have an axe/ax to grind *eigennützige Zwecke verfolgen (eine Axt zu schärfen haben)*

A

back
to get off someone's back *jn. in Ruhe lassen*
to stab someone in the back *jn. hintergehen/in den Rücken fallen*

backseat
to take a backseat to *die zweite Geige spielen*

bad
to go from bad to worse *noch schlechter werden*

bag
in the bag *unter Dach und Fach haben* **133/134**

ball
to have a ball *sich köstlich amüsieren*
to have the ball in one's court *am Zug sein*

bandwagon
to jump on the bandwagon *mit den Wölfen heulen*

bargain
to drive a hard bargain *mit harten Bandagen kämpfen; knallhart verhandeln* **131**
to get more than one bargained for *mehr als erwartet bekommen* **124**
to strike a bargain *etwas aushandeln; eine Abmachung treffen* **67/68**

bark
His bark is worse than his bite. [*] *Hunde, die bellen, beißen nicht.* **5/6**

bat
as blind as a bat *blind wie eine Fledermaus* **129**
to have bats in the belfry *einen Vogel haben*

bathroom
to have to go to the bathroom *aufs Klo müssen* **107**

beans
to spill the beans *ein Geheimnis preisgeben* **21/22/91**

beauty
Beauty is in the eye of the beholder. [*] *Schönheit existiert (nur) im Auge des Betrachters.*
Beauty is only skin deep. [*] *Schönheit ist nur an der Oberfläche.*

beck
at someone's beck and call *jm. auf den leisesten Wink gehorchen*

bed
to get out of bed on the wrong side *auf dem falschen Fuß aufstehen*
to have made one's bed and have to lie in it *die Suppe, die man sich eingebrockt hat, auslöffeln müssen*

beeline
to make a beeline for *auf etwas zustürzen*

beggars
Beggars can't be choosers. [*] *Du kannst es dir nicht leisten, wählerisch zu sein.*

belt
to hit below the belt *unter die Gürtellinie schlagen*
to tighten one's belt *den Gürtel enger schnallen*

bend
to bend over backwards *sich ein Bein ausreißen (um jn. zufrieden zu stellen)*

benefit
to give someone the benefit of the doubt *den vorhandenen Zweifel zu js. Gunsten auslegen*

best
to be all for the best *wirklich gar nicht so schlimm sein*
32/40

between
This is just between you and me. *Das bleibt unter uns.*

B

bird
Birds of a feather flock together. [*] *Gleich und gleich gesellt sich gern*
The early bird catches the worm. [*] *Morgenstund' hat Gold im Mund.*
to kill two birds with one stone *zwei Fliegen mit einer Klappe schlagen* **1/2/149**

biscuit
to take the biscuit/to take the cake *der letzte Heuler sein*

bite
to bite off more than one can chew *mehr in Angriff nehmen, als man bewältigen kann* **31/32**

blessing
a blessing in disguise *Glück im Unglück*
a mixed blessing *ein zweischneidiges Schwert; eine zweischneidige Sache* **147/148**
to count one's blessings *dankbar sein für das, was man hat*

blind
the blind leading the blind *Unbedarfte, die anderen Unbedarften etwas erklären; hoffnungsloser Versuch*

blood
Blood is thicker than water. [*] *Gegenüber den Blutsverwandten loyal sein. (Blut ist dicker als Wasser.)*
to make someone's blood boil *js. Blut zum Wallen bringen*
to sweat blood *Blut und Wasser schwitzen*

blue
out of the blue *aus heiterem Himmel*

bluff
to call someone's bluff *jn. auffordern, es doch zu tun; jn. auffliegen lassen*

body
Over my dead body. [*] *Nur über meine Leiche.*

bombshell
to drop a bombshell *eine Nachricht, die wie eine Bombe einschlägt, verkünden* **34**

bone
to have a bone to pick with someone *ein Hühnchen mit jm. zu rupfen haben*

book
not to judge a book by its cover *nicht aufgrund von Äußerlichkeiten urteilen, der Schein könnte trügen* **137/138**

bottle
to hit the bottle *saufen* **55**

bottom
from the bottom of one's heart *von ganzem Herzen*

brain
to rack one's brains *sich den Kopf zerbrechen*

bread
to earn one's daily bread *sein täglich Brot verdienen* **15**

break
Give me a break! [*] *Jetzt mach mal halblang!* **4**

breath
to waste one's breath *unnütz Worte machen*

bridge
to cross a bridge when one comes to it *alles zu seiner Zeit (die Brücke überqueren, wenn man bei ihr ankommt)*

bucket
to kick the bucket *sterben; den Löffel aus der Hand legen* **127/128**

bud
to nip something in the bud *etwas im Keim ersticken* **81/82**

bull
to hit the bull's eye *den Nagel auf den Kopf treffen*
to take the bull by the horns *den Stier bei den Hörnern packen* **9/10**

bullet
to bite the bullet *die Zähne zusammenbeißen; etwas durchstehen; tapfer sein* **139/140**

bump
to bump/run into someone *jn. zufällig treffen*

bush
to beat around/about the bush *nicht zur Sache kommen; wie die Katze um den heißen Brei herumschleichen* **93/94/110/153**

business
Business before pleasure. [*] *Erst die Arbeit, dann das Vergnügen.*
to get down to business *eine Sache in Angriff nehmen* **123**
to mean business *es wirklich ernst meinen* **6**
to mind one's own business *sich um seine eigenen Angelegenheiten kümmern* **63/64**

butter
to butter someone up *jm. Honig ums Maul schmieren* **39/40**
butterfingers *ungeschickte Person; Tollpatsch*

butterflies
to have butterflies in one's stomach *nervös sein*

cake
to eat one's cake and have it too *man kann nicht alles haben, man muss sich entscheiden* **23/24**

call
That was a close call. *Das was aber knapp.*

candle
not fit to hold a candle to *jm. nicht das Wasser reichen können*

to burn the candle at both ends *die eigenen Kräfte überfordern*

card
to play one's cards right *klug (ver)handeln*
to put one's cards on the table *die Karten auf den Tisch legen*

case
to be the case *zutreffen; der Fall sein* **91**

cash
to be a little short on cash *ein bisschen knapp bei Kasse sein* **42**
to cash in on something *von etwas profitieren*

castles
to build castles in the air *Luftschlösser bauen* **45**

cat
to let the cat out of the bag *die Katze aus dem Sack lassen*
to rain cats and dogs *in Strömen gießen* **117**
When the cat's away, the mice will play. [*] *Wenn die Katze aus dem Haus ist, tanzen die Mäuse auf dem Tisch.*

catch
to catch someone red-handed *jn. auf frischer Tat ertappen* **134**
to catch up with someone *jn. einholen* **13/117**

ceiling
to hit the ceiling *in die Luft gehen* **41**

cent
not to have a red cent *keinen roten Heller besitzen* **65**

chance
to take a chance *etwas riskieren* **50/78**

change
a change of scenery *Tapetenwechsel* **158**

charge
to be in charge *verantwortlich sein* **152**

check
to check someone out *sich jn. mal genauer anschauen* **2/158**
to check something out *etwas prüfen; etwas ausleihen* **142**

cheer
Cheer up! [*] *Sei nicht so verbissen!* **105/156**

chest
to get something off one's chest *sich etwas von der Seele schaffen* **153**

chickens
to count one's chickens before they hatch *das Fell des Bären verkaufen, ehe man ihn hat*

child
to father a child *ein Kind zeugen* **51**

chin
to keep one's chin up *die Ohren steif halten*

chip
a chip off the old block *ganz der Vater sein* **121/122**
to have a chip on one's shoulder *vor Zorn geladen sein*

clear
to clear out *sich dünnmachen* **139**

clockwork
like clockwork *wie am Schnürchen*

closet
to come out of the closet *sich selbst offen zu etwas bekennen; sich «outen»* **155**

cloud
Every cloud has a silver lining. [*] *Jedes Unglück hat auch seine guten Seiten.*
to be on cloud nine *im siebten Himmel sein*

club
Join the club! [*] *Jetzt hat's dich auch erwischt, willkommen im Club!*

clue
not to have a clue *keine Ahnung haben*

coast
The coast is clear. [*] *Die Luft ist rein.*

collar
to get hot under the collar *wütend werden*

color
to show one's true colors *sein wahres Gesicht zeigen*
with flying colors *mit fliegenden Fahnen; erfolgreich*

come
when it comes to ... *was ... angeht/betrifft* **42**

company
to keep someone company *jm. Gesellschaft leisten*
Two's company, three's a crowd. [*] *Drei sind einer zu viel.* **160**

concerned
to be concerned about *sich Sorgen machen um* **48**

conclusions
to jump to conclusions *voreilige Schlüsse ziehen* **86**

cook
Too many cooks spoil the broth/soup. [*] *Viele Köche verderben den Brei.*

cookie
That's the way the cookie crumbles. [*] *Da liegt der Hase im Pfeffer; so sieht's aus.*

corner
to cut corners *etwas beschleunigen, indem man es nachlässiger ausführt*

crack
This isn't all it's cracked up to be. *Es ist nicht so gut, wie alle gesagt haben.*
to crack down on *scharf vorgehen gegen* **77**

C

cream
the cream of the crop *der/das Allerbeste, allererste Sahne* **25/26**

creek
to be up the creek (without a paddle) *in Schwierigkeiten stecken, ohne dass sich eine Lösung anbietet* **85/86**

creeps
the creeps *Gruseln; Gänsehaut* **153/154**

crowd
Three's a crowd. [*] *Drei sind einer zu viel.* **160**

cup
to be one's cup of tea *js. Berufung/Lieblingsbeschäftigung sein; jm. liegen* **37/38**

curiosity
Curiosity killed the cat. [*] *Sei nicht so neugierig. (Die Neugierde tötete die Katze.)*

cut
a cut above *besser als alles andere*
not to be cut out for something *nicht dazu geschaffen sein*
to cut it out *aufhören mit*

damn
not to be worth a damn *keinen Pfifferling wert sein*
not to give a damn *sich einen Dreck drum scheren* **151/152**

dawn
to dawn on someone *etwas dämmert einem; jm. geht ein Licht auf* **22**

day
not to be one's day *einen schlechten Tag haben* **117/118**
That'll be the day! [*] *Nie im Leben! Das ist äußerst unwahrscheinlich.* **105/106**
Those were the days. [*] *Das waren noch Zeiten.*
to call it a day *für heute Schluss machen*
to have seen better days *bessere Zeiten gesehen haben*

to make one's day *jn. glücklich machen; js. Tag retten* **103/104**
to save something for a rainy day *etwas auf die hohe Kante legen*

dead
to be dead set on something *sich auf etwas versteifen*

deal
to make a big deal about something *wegen etwas ein Riesentheater machen* **139**

death
You look like death warmed up/over. *Du siehst aus wie zwischen achtzig und scheintot.*

degree
to give (someone) the third degree *jn. ins Kreuzverhör nehmen* **128**

desire
to leave much to be desired *viel zu wünschen übrig lassen*

doctor
just what the doctor ordered *genau, was man braucht*

dog
Let sleeping dogs lie. [*] *Schlafende Hunde soll man nicht wecken.* **7/8**
to go to the dogs *vor die Hunde gehen*
to lead a dog's life *ein Hundeleben führen*
You can't teach an old dog new tricks. [*] *Was Hänschen nicht lernt, lernt Hans nimmermehr.* **19/20**

done
to be done for *erledigt sein* **16**

dose
to give someone a dose of his own medicine *jn. mit seinen eigenen Waffen schlagen* **100**

downhill
to go downhill *den Bach runtergehen; versacken; sich verschlimmern* **150**

drain
down the drain *den Bach runtergehen* **131/132**

drawing board
to go back to the drawing board *wieder von vorn beginnen*

drift
to get the drift *verstehen, worauf jemand hinauswill*

driving
to be driving at *hinauswollen auf*

drop
a drop in the bucket/ocean *ein Tropfen auf dem heißen Stein*

drown
to drown one's sorrows *seinen Kummer im Alkohol ertränken*

duckling
an ugly duckling *hässliches Entlein*

dump
a dump *ein mieses Loch* **88/146**

dust
to bite the dust *ins Gras beißen*

dying
to be dying to *kaum erwarten können* **123**

E

ear
to be all ears *ganz Ohr sein*
to be wet behind the ears *noch nicht trocken hinter den Ohren sein*
to go in one ear and out the other *rein ins eine Ohr, raus aus dem anderen*

to play it by ear *improvisieren*
up to one's ears *bis über beide Ohren*

easy
Easier said than done. [*] *Leichter gesagt als getan.*
Easy come, easy go. [*] *Wie gewonnen, so zerronnen.*
to go easy on someone *nicht so streng mit jm. sein*

edge
to be on edge *angespannt sein* **32**

egg
to egg someone on *anstacheln, aufhetzen*
to have egg on one's face *ins Fettnäpfchen treten*
to put all one's eggs in one basket *alles auf eine Karte setzen*

elbow
to rub elbows/shoulders *am gleichen Ort sein, in Kontakt kommen* **45/46/47**

else
or else *oder es passiert was* **6**

end
not to let someone hear the end of this *jm. keine Ruhe mehr geben; etwas immer wieder erwähnen* **131**
to go off the deep end *ausrasten*
to make ends meet *finanziell über die Runden kommen* **40/61/62**
to put an end to *beenden; kurzen Prozess machen* **75/89**

equal
to treat someone as an equal *jn. wie seinesgleichen behandeln* **47**

even
to break even *ohne Gewinn oder Verlust abschließen; die Gewinnzone erreichen*
to get even with someone *es jm. heimzahlen*

E

example
to set an example *ein Vorbild sein*

eye
not to bat an eyelid *nicht mal mit der Wimper zucken*
not to be able to believe one's eyes/ears *seinen Augen/Ohren nicht trauen* **33**
There's more to that than meets the eye. [*] *Es gibt mehr, als man mit bloßem Auge sehen kann.*
to keep an eye on something *auf etwas aufpassen*
to keep one's eyes peeled *die Augen offen halten; genau beobachten*
to lay eyes on ... *... betrachten* **135**
to see eye to eye with someone *mit jm. übereinstimmen*

far
by far *bei weitem* **56**
So far, so good. [*] *So weit, so gut.*

favor
to ask a favor *um einen Gefallen bitten* **155**

feathers
to ruffle someone's feathers *jn. vergrätzen, verärgern* **3/4/37**

fed
to be fed up with something *etwas satt haben* **10**

feet
to be on one's feet again *wieder auf den Beinen sein; alles abgeklärt haben* **13**
to get cold feet *kalte Füße kriegen* **36**
to stand on one's own two feet *auf eigenen Füßen stehen*
to sweep someone off his/her feet *js. Herz im Sturm erobern*

fiddle
as fit as a fiddle *kerngesund* **101**
to fiddle around with *rummachen mit*
to play second fiddle (to someone) *die zweite Geige spielen (nach jm.)*

fight
to pick a fight *Streit suchen* **7**

figure
to figure something out *etwas verstehen* **24**
That figures. [*] *Das sieht ihm ähnlich; das ist genau, was ich erwartet habe.*

find
Finders, keepers. [*] *Was man gefunden hat, darf man behalten.*

finger
not to lift a finger *keinen Finger krumm machen*
to have at one's fingertips *in Reichweite/parat haben*
to have green fingers/a green thumb *ein Händchen für Pflanzen haben*
to keep one's fingers crossed *jm. die Daumen drücken* **49/50**
to point the finger at *jm. die Schuld geben*
to twist/wrap someone around one's little finger *jn. um den Finger wickeln*
to work one's fingers to the bone *sich kaputtarbeiten* **62**

fire
to play with fire *mit dem Feuer spielen*
to spread like wildfire *sich wie ein Lauffeuer verbreiten*

fish
There's plenty more fish in the sea. [*] *Es gibt noch viele andere Möglichkeiten.*
to be fishy *einem spanisch vorkommen*
to drink like a fish *saufen*

flesh
one's own flesh and blood *js. eigen Fleisch und Blut* **5**

fly
He wouldn't hurt a fly. *Er würde keiner Fliege etwas zuleide tun.* **138**
I would like to be a fly on the wall. *Dort möchte ich Mäuschen sein.*
to zip one's fly *den Hosenlatz schließen* **22**

F

follow
I don't follow you. *Ich kann dir nicht ganz folgen.* **147**

fool
to fool around with *rummachen mit* **28/36**
to make a fool of someone/oneself *sich zum Narren machen*

foot
to follow in someone's footsteps *in js. Fußstapfen treten* **49**
to get cold feet *kalte Füße bekommen* **36**
to get off on the wrong foot *einen schlechten Start haben*
to have one foot in the grave *mit einem Bein im Grab stehen*
to put one's foot down *einen festen Standpunkt einnehmen; seine Meinung klar machen* **138**
to put one's foot in one's mouth/it *ins Fettnäpfchen treten*

frog
to have a frog in one's throat *einen Frosch im Hals haben*

fun
to be no fun to be around someone *keinen Spaß daran haben, mit jm. zusammen zu sein* **152**
to make/poke fun of someone *sich über jm. lustig machen*

fuss
to make a fuss over *Theater machen wegen; sich übertriebene Umstände machen*

games
to play games with *mit jm. sein Spielchen treiben* **89**

gang
to gang up on someone *sich zusammenrotten gegen*

get
I get it! *Jetzt kapiere ich's!* **96**
to get away from it all *sich (auf die Insel) absetzen*
to get of scot-free *ungeschoren davonkommen* **138**
to get something off the ground *loslegen; mit etwas beginnen*

gift
He thinks he is God's gift to women. *Was seine Wirkung auf Frauen angeht, ist er sehr von sich eingenommen. (Er denkt, er sei Gottes Geschenk an die Frauen.)*

glimpse
to catch a glimpse of *einen flüchtigen Blick erhaschen von* **76**

go
at one go *auf einen Schlag; mit nur einem Versuch*
Go ahead! *Mach doch, los geht's!* **159**
it goes without saying that *es ist selbstverständlich, dass*
There goes my ...! *Mein ... ist futsch!* **30**
to be on the go *auf Achse sein*
to go over something *etwas durchsprechen* **27**
to have a go *einen Versuch machen/wagen*
What's going on? *Was geht denn hier vor?* **141**

goat
to get someone's goat *jn. auf die Palme bringen*

good
a good-for-nothing *Taugenichts* **44**
as good as new *so gut wie neu* **120**
Good for you. *Schön für dich. Gut gemacht.* **38**
not to do much good *nicht viel nützen* **21**
to be half as good as *auch nur halb so gut sein wie* **147**
to be up to no good *etwas im Schilde führen*

grade
to make the grade *Erfolg haben; einen bestimmten Standard erreichen*

grain
to go against someone's grain *jm. gegen den Strich gehen*
with a grain of a salt *unter Vorbehalt*

grant
to take for granted *als selbstverständlich betrachten*

grapevine
through/from the grapevine *vom Hörensagen; durch Gerüchte*

grass
The grass is always greener on the other side (of the fence). [*] *Was man bereits hat, ist nie gut genug. (Auf der anderen Seite des Zauns ist das Gras immer grüner.)*

grave
to turn in one's grave *sich im Grabe umdrehen*

Greek
It's all Greek to me. *Ich verstehe nur Bahnhof.*

grin
to grin and bear it *gute Miene zum bösen Spiel machen*

grip
to come to grips with *mit etwas zurechtkommen; etwas in den Griff kriegen*
to get a grip on oneself *sich zusammenreißen*

ground
to hold/stand one's ground *sich behaupten*
to get something off the ground *loslegen; mit etwas beginnen*

grow
to grow on someone *jm. ans Herz wachsen* **71**

guard
to be on one's guard *auf der Hut sein*

guest
Be my guest. [*] *Bedien dich; nimm dir, was du brauchst.* **114/159/160**

gun
to jump the gun *voreilig sein; einen Fehlstart verursachen*
to stick to one's guns *nicht nachgeben*

guts
to have guts *Mut haben (Därme haben)* **139**
to hate someone's guts *jn. inbrünstig hassen*

hair
to split hairs *Haarspalterei betreiben*

half
to be half as good as *auch nur halb so gut sein wie* **147**
to meet someone halfway *einen Kompromiss treffen*

hand
hands down *mit links; ohne Anstrengung*
single-handed *ohne fremde Hilfe*
to bite the hand that feeds one *den Ast absägen, auf dem man sitzt*
to get one's hands on *etwas in die Finger kriegen* **130**
to get out of hand *außer Kontrolle geraten* **22/151**
to give someone a (helping) hand *jm. helfen*
to have one's hands full *alle Hände voll zu tun haben* **126**
to live from hand to mouth *von der Hand in den Mund leben*
to raise a hand against *die Hand erheben gegen* **5**
to try one's hand at something *sein Glück mit etwas versuchen*
to wash one's hands of something *seine Hände in Unschuld waschen*
to win hands down *ohne Anstrengung gewinnen*

handle
to fly off the handle *die Fassung verlieren; fuchsteufelswild werden* **129/130**
to handle something *etwas schaffen* **27/31**

handy
to come in handy *gelegen kommen*

hang
to get the hang/swing of something *etwas in den Griff kriegen*

happy
to be happy for someone *sich für jn. freuen* **145**

harp
to harp on something *herumreiten auf etwas*

hat
to keep something under one's hat *etwas für sich behalten*

H

have
to have had it *etwas satt haben* **10/112**
have to have it in for someone *es auf jn. abgesehen haben*
have to have what it takes *geeignet sein*
have to let someone have it *jm. eine Abreibung verpassen*

hay
to go haywire *durcheinander geraten*
to hit the hay *sich aufs Ohr legen*

head
head over heels in love *bis über beide Ohren verliebt* **3/47/48**
not to be able to make head or tail of *aus etwas nicht schlau werden können*
off the top of one's head *ohne viel zu überlegen*
sleepy head *Schlafmütze* **101**
to be over someone's head *js. Fähigkeiten übersteigen; jn. überfordern*
to bite someone's head off *jn. ausschimpfen*
to go to someone's head *jm. zu Kopfe steigen*
to have a good head on one's shoulders *ein kluger Kopf sein*
to have one's head in the clouds *im siebten Himmel sein*
to head for ... *Richtung ... fahren* **13/109**
to keep a cool head *einen kühlen Kopf bewahren* **130**
to keep one's head above water *den Kopf über Wasser halten*
to put our heads together *die Köpfe zusammenstecken*

heart
by heart *auswendig*
My heart is not in it. *Ich bin nicht mit ganzem Herzen dabei.*
My heart stood still. *Mir stand das Herz still.* **47**
not to have the heart to do something *nicht den Mut haben, etwas zu tun*
to have a change of heart *die Meinung ändern*
to have one's heart in the right place *das Herz am rechten Fleck tragen*
to have one's heart set on something *das Herz an etwas hängen* **101**
to steal someone's heart *js. Herz stehlen* **15**

heaven
in seventh heaven *im siebten Himmel* **145**
to blow to high heaven *in die Luft blasen/sprengen* **110**
to stink to high heaven *zum Himmel stinken*

heck
a/one heck/hell of a ... *ein Wahnsinns...* **19**
who the heck/hell *wer zum Teufel* **89**

heel
to dig in one's heels *nicht von der Stelle weichen; auf etwas beharren*

hell
All hell broke loose. [*] *Die Hölle war los.*
come hell or high water *egal, welche Schwierigkeiten auch überwunden werden müssen* **97/98**
just for the hell of it *nur zum Spaß; aus Jux und Dollerei* **155/156**
to give someone hell *jn. fertig machen*
What the hell! [*] *Was soll's?*
when hell freezes over *nie und nimmer* **119/120**

hill
over the hill *die besten Jahre hinter sich habend*
to go downhill *den Bach runtergehen; versacken; sich verschlimmern* **150**

hint
to get/take the hint *den zarten Hinweis verstehen* **139**

hit
to hit it off *sich auf Anhieb gut verstehen*

hole
to burn a hole in someone's pocket *(Geld) ausgeben wollen*

home
nothing to write home about *nichts besonders Großartiges*
to bring home the bacon *die Brötchen nach Hause bringen; den Lebensunterhalt verdienen* **35/36/40**

to do one's homework *sich gut vorbereiten*
to make oneself at home *es sich bequem machen*

hook
to get/let someone off the hook *jn. loseisen/laufen lassen* **138**

horse
Hold your horses! *Immer mit der Ruhe!*
straight from the horse's mouth *etwas brühwarm erzählt bekommen; etwas aus erster Hand erfahren* **17/18**
to look a gift horse in the mouth *einem geschenkten Gaul ins Maul schauen*
Wild horses would not make me do it! *Keine zehn Pferde würden mich dazu bringen!*
You can lead a horse to water but you can't make it drink. [*] *Man kann jn. nur ermutigen, handeln muss er aber schließlich selbst. (Du kannst ein Pferd ans Wasser führen, aber es nicht zum Trinken zwingen.)*

hour
after hours *nach Geschäftsschluss* **55**
an ungodly hour *unchristlich frühe Stunde* **117**

house
to eat someone out of house and home *jm. die Haare vom Kopf fressen* **61**

hush
hush money *Schmiergeld*
to hush something up *etwas unter den Tisch kehren*

ice
to be skating on thin ice *ein heikles Thema anschneiden/besprechen*
to put something on ice *etwas auf Eis legen*

I

idea
not to have the faintest idea *nicht die leiseste Ahnung haben* **97**

image
to be the spitting image of someone *jm. wie aus dem Gesicht geschnitten sein*

impression
to be under the impression that *den Eindruck haben, dass*

in
There's ... in it for you. *Du kannst dir ... dazuverdienen.* **87**
to be in on something *eingeweiht sein in*

inch
Give him an inch and he'll take a mile. *Wenn man jm. den kleinen Finger gibt, wird gleich die ganze Hand genommen.*
to inch closer to *näher rücken an* **9**

insult
to add insult to injury *Wer den Schaden hat, braucht für den Spott nicht zu sorgen. (zur Verletzung auch noch die Beleidigung hinzufügen)* **34**

involve
to be involved with someone *mit jm. eine Beziehung haben* **83**

jack
a jack-of-all-trades *Hansdampf in allen Gassen*

jackpot
to hit the jackpot *das große Los ziehen; Riesenerfolg haben* **69/70**

jiffy
in a jiffy *im Nu*

jitters
to give one the jitters *jn. nervös machen* **6**

job
a lousy job *äußerst dürftige Leistung* **120**

judge
to let someone be the judge *jn. selbst bewerten/entscheiden lassen* **61**

J

juice
to stew in one's own juice *im eigenen Saft schmoren*

jungle
It's a jungle out there. *Das draußen geht's wüst zu.* **2**

keel
to keel over *plötzlich umfallen (kentern)*

keep
to keep at it/it up *weitermachen; nicht aufgeben*
to keep something to oneself *etwas für sich behalten* **44**
to work for one's keep *für Kost und Logis arbeiten; sich bezahlt machen* **60**

kick
for kicks *zum Spaß*
to kick oneself *sich in den Hintern beißen*

kill
to kill someone *jn. fertig machen* **7**
to make a killing *ein Haufen Geld verdienen*

knee
to bring someone to his knees *jn. in die Knie zwingen*

knock
Knock it off! *Schluss damit!* **139**
Knock on/touch wood! [*] *Toi, toi, toi!*

know
for all I know *soweit ich weiß*
to know something backwards/inside out *etwas in- und auswendig kennen*
You never know. *Man weiß ja nie (..., was noch alles möglich ist).*

knuckle
to knuckle under *nachgeben; sich einer stärkeren Macht unterwerfen* **53/54**

landslide
to win by a landslide *mit überwältigender Mehrheit gewinnen*

last
at last *endlich* **74**

laugh
no laughing matter *nichts, was man auf die leichte Schulter nehmen könnte*
to have the last laugh *am Ende doch noch triumphieren (den letzten Lacher haben)*
to laugh something off *etwas mit einem Lachen abtun*

lead
to lead someone on *falsche Hoffnungen wecken*

lead
to pump someone full of lead *jn. umlegen* **10**

leaf
to turn over a new leaf *von neuem beginnen (ein neues Blatt aufschlagen)*

least
the least I can do *das Mindeste, was ich tun kann* **114**

leg
not to have a leg to stand on *keinerlei Beweise haben*
to be on one's last legs *aus dem letzten Loch pfeifen*
to pull someone's leg *jn. einen Bären aufbinden; jn. veräppeln* **51/52/102**
to stretch one's legs *sich die Beine vertreten* **109**

lengths
to go to any lengths *alles Erdenkliche tun*

leper
to treat someone like a leper *jn. wie einen Aussätzigen behandeln* **131**

L

let
to let/leave well enough alone *was gut genug ist, nicht weiter verbessern*

liberty
at liberty to do something *etwas tun dürfen*

lid
to blow the lid off something *(z. B. einen Skandal) aufdecken*

life
to last a lifetime *genug für ein ganzes Leben sein* **20**
to make someone's life miserable *jm. das Leben vermiesen* **10**
to take one's life in one's own hands *sein Leben aufs Spiel setzen*

light
to hide one's light under a bushel *js. Licht unter den Scheffel stellen*
to shed light on something *Licht werfen auf*

lightning
as quick as lightning *blitzschnell*
Lightning never strikes in the same place twice. *Ungewöhnliche Unfälle wiederholen sich nicht. (Der Blitz schlägt nie zweimal an derselben Stelle ein.)*
like greased lightning *wie ein geölter Blitz*

like
This isn't like you. *Das sieht dir aber überhaupt nicht ähnlich.* **141**
the likes of *so etwas wie; solche wie*

limb
to be out on a limb *sich in einer gefährlichen Lage befinden*

limelight
in the limelight *im Rampenlicht*

line
to draw the line *die Grenze ziehen; Halt machen*
to read between the lines *zwischen den Zeilen lesen*
to sign on the dotted line *unterschreiben*
to step out of line *aus der Rolle fallen; seine Grenzen überschreiten*

lip
to keep a stiff upper lip *die Ohren steif halten; sich nicht entmutigen lassen* **57/58**
to play lip-service to something *ein Lippenbekenntnis ablegen zu etwas*

load
to take/get a load off one's mind *jm. eine Last von der Seele nehmen*

lock
lock, stock and barrel *komplett*
under lock and key *hinter Schloss und Riegel*

log
to sleep like a log *tief und fest schlafen*

look
not to give someone a second look *jn. keines zweiten Blickes würdigen* **135**
to get a closer look *sich etwas aus der Nähe anschauen*
to look someone up and down *jn. genau inspizieren*

losses
to cut one's losses *seine Verluste begrenzen*

love
There's no love lost between them. *Sie haben nichts für einander übrig.*

luck
one's lucky day *js. Glückstag*
to be plain lucky *einfach nur Glück gehabt haben* **70**
to push one's luck *sein Schicksal herausfordern*
to try one's luck at ... *sein Glück mit ... versuchen* **49**
Who's the lucky person? *Wer ist denn die Glückliche?* **145**

lump
If you don't like it, you can lump it. *Wenn dir's nicht passt, kannst du's ja bleiben lassen.*

lung
at the top of one's lungs *aus vollem Halse (schreien)* **38**

make
to have the makings of ... *das Zeug zu ... haben*
to make do with something *mit etwas auskommen*
to make it to ... *es bis nach ... schaffen* **13**
to make up for something *etwas wieder gutmachen*

man
a man after one's own heart *ein Mann ganz nach seinem/ihrem Geschmack* **10**
Every man for himself. [*] *Jeder kämpft für sich allein.*

mark
to make one's mark *einen bleibenden Eindruck hinterlassen*

match
to be a match for someone *jm. gewachsen sein*
to meet one's match *seinen Meister finden*

matter
It's a matter of life and death. *Es geht um Leben oder Tod.* **155**
a matter of opinion *Geschmackssache/Anschauungssache*

mean
by all/no means *auf jeden/keinen Fall*

memory
if my memory serves me right *wenn ich mich richtig erinnere*
to refresh one's memory *sein Gedächtnis auffrischen*

mention
not to mention *ganz zu schweigen von*

mercy
to be at the mercy of someone *jm. auf Gedeih und Verderb ausgeliefert sein*

message
to get the message *etwas kapieren*

middle
in the middle of nowhere *am Ende der Welt; in einer gottverlassenen Gegend* **114**

midnight
to burn the midnight oil *bis tief in die Nacht arbeiten* **101/102**

midstream
to stop in midstream *mitten in einer Tätigkeit (beim Sprechen) innehalten*

mile
to stick out a mile *ganz offensichtlich sein*

milk
to cry over spilled milk *passiert ist passiert, hin ist hin* **12/29/30**

mincemeat
to make mincemeat of someone *aus jm. Hackfleisch machen*

mind
Great minds think alike. [*] *Große Geister denken gleich.*
in one's right mind *bei klarem Verstand; im Vollbesitz seiner geistigen Kräfte* **52**
to be out of one's mind *übergeschnappt sein* **28/70/131**
to be scared out of one's mind *völlig verängstigt sein; Panik kriegen*
to change one's mind *es sich anders überlegen*
to cross one's mind *jm. in den Sinn kommen*
to have a one-track mind *immer nur dasselbe (Sex!) im Kopf haben*
to have someone/something in mind *schon wissen, wer/was* **149**

M

to keep an open mind *sich anderer Leute Vorschläge und Ideen vorbehaltlos anhören*
to lose one's mind *seinen Verstand verlieren* **101**
to make up one's mind *einen Entschluss fassen*
to put someone's mind at rest *jn. beruhigen*
to slip one's mind *aus dem Gedächtnis entgleiten; entfallen*
to speak one's mind *aus seinem Herzen keine Mördergrube machen; Klartext reden*
to take one's mind off *jn. auf andere Gedanken bringen* **1**

mint
in mint condition *nagelneu*

mint
to make a mint *einen Haufen Geld verdienen*

mischief
to get into mischief *etwas «anstellen»* **122**

moment
in the heat of the moment *im Eifer des Gefechts*
on the spur of the moment *ohne Überlegung; spontan*

money
Money doesn't grow on trees. [*] *Geld wächst nicht auf Bäumen.*
Money is no object. [*] *Geld spielt keine Rolle.* **77/78**
to get one's money's worth *etwas für sein Geld bekommen*
to have money to burn *Geld wie Heu haben*
to put one's money where one's mouth is *den Worten (finanzielle) Taten folgen lassen* **73/74**
to throw money out of the window *Geld zum Fenster rausschmeißen* **80**

moon
as if I had fallen off the moon *als wäre ich vom Mond gefallen* **22**
once in a blue moon *alle Jubeljahre einmal*

most
to make the most of something *das Beste aus etwas herausholen*

motions
to go through the motions *etwas völlig lustlos betreiben* **143/144**

mountain
to make a mountain out of a molehill *aus einer Mücke einen Elefanten machen*

mourning
to go into mourning *trauern* **15**

mouth
to have a big mouth *ein Klatschmaul haben* **24**
to shoot one's mouth off *blöd quatschen*

move
to get a move on *einen Zahn zulegen; sich beeilen*
to move in with someone *zu jm. in die Wohnung ziehen* **144**

murder
to get away with murder *ohne Strafe davonkommen*

music
to face the music *die Suppe auslöffeln*

nail
as hard as nails *eisern; unbarmherzig*
to hit the nail on the head *den Nagel auf den Kopf treffen* **123/124**

neck
to be in up to one's neck in *bis über beide Ohren in etwas stecken*
to breathe down someone's neck *jm. im Nacken sitzen* **8**
to risk one's neck *Kopf und Kragen riskieren*
to stick one's neck out *für jn. den Kopf hinhalten*

needle
like looking for a needle in a haystack *als ob man eine Nadel im Heuhaufen sucht* **125/126**

nerve
to have the nerve to do something *den Mut/die Frechheit besitzen, etwas zu tun*
to get on someone's nerves *jm. auf die Nerven gehen*
25/148/152

news
No news is good news. [*] *Wenn man nichts von einem hört, so heißt das, dass es ihm gut geht. (Keine Neuigkeiten sind gute Neuigkeiten.)*
That's news to me. *Das ist mir neu.*
to break the news *eine (meist traurige) Nachricht mitteilen* **51**

next
next to nothing *fast gar nichts*

nick
in the nick of time *keine Sekunde zu spät; gerade noch recht-zeitig* **109/110**

night
like night and day *(unterschiedlich) wie Tag und Nacht* **3**
to make a night of it *sich die Nacht um die Ohren schlagen*

nit
nit-picking *kleinliche Korinthenkackerei (Nissen suchen)*
to get down to the nitty-gritty *die eigentliche Sache anpacken*

No
No way/go! [*] *Niemals!* **28/39/67**

nose
to follow one's nose *immer der Nase nach gehen*
to keep one's nose clean *sich aus etwas heraushalten*
to keep one's nose to the grindstone *sich schinden; schuften*
to lead someone by the nose *jn. völlig kontrollieren*
to look down one's nose at *jn. verachten; auf jn. herabschau-en* **43/44**
to pay through the nose *einen Haufen Geld blechen*
to poke one's nose into something *seine Nase in etwas stecken*

to rub someone's nose in it *jn. mit der Nase auf etwas stoßen; jn. an etwas erinnern*
to turn up one's nose at something *die Nase über etwas rümpfen*

Nothing
Nothing doing! [*] *Das kommt gar nicht in Frage!*
There's nothing to it. [*] *Das ist kinderleicht.*

nuts
in a nutshell *in aller Kürze*
to be nuts *total verrückt sein* **39/156**

oats
to sow one's wild oats *sich die Hörner abstoßen; über die Stränge schlagen* **83/84**

odds
odds and ends *Krimskrams; Sammelsurium; Kleinigkeiten*

oil
to pour oil on troubled waters *die Gemüter beruhigen (Öl auf stürmisches Wasser gießen)*

once
to give someone the once-over *jn. kurz mustern*

open
open and shut *offensichtlich*

opportunity
a golden opportunity *eine gute Gelegenheit*

option
to keep one's options open *nach allen Seiten offen bleiben; sich nicht festlegen*

order
in good working order *voll betriebsfähig* **85**
out of order *defekt*

ordinary
out of the ordinary *etwas Ungewöhnliches*

O

overboard
to go overboard *übertreiben* **71**

overdo
to overdo it *überbeanspruchen; übertreiben*

own
to hold one's own *sich behaupten*

paces
to put one through one's paces *jn./etwas auf seine Belastbarkeit testen* **11/12**

pain
a pain in the ass/neck *eine Nervensäge* **41/42**
to take pains *sich Mühe geben*

palm
to grease someone's palm *jn. bestechen (die Handfläche schmieren)* **18**
to have someone in the palm of one's hand *jn. in der Hand haben*

pants
to be caught with one's pants down *auf frischer Tat ertappt werden*
to drop one's pants *die Hosen runterlassen* **93**
to wear the pants in one's house *zu Hause die Hosen anhaben* **95**
to wet one's pants *sich in die Hosen machen*

par
not up to par/below par *keine Konkurrenz darstellen*
That was par for the course. *Damit hatten wir schon gerechnet.*

pass
to make a pass at someone *einer Person gegenüber zudringlich werden; jn. anmachen*
to pass as *durchgehen als*
to pass away *verscheiden; sterben*
to pass off as *sich ausgeben als*
to pass something up *verzichten auf*

pat
a pat on the back *Lob (Schulterklopfen)*

pea
like two peas in a pod *sich wie ein Ei dem anderen gleichen*

peace
to disturb the peace *öffentliches Ärgernis erregen* **18**
to have a little peace and quiet *Ruhe haben* **42**

pearls
to throw pearls before the swine *Perlen vor die Säue werfen*

pedestal
to put someone on a pedestal *jn. auf ein Podest erheben*

peek
to take a peek *einen Blick werfen* **48**

peg
to take someone down a peg *jn. auf seine normale Größe zurechtstutzen*

penny
A penny for your thoughts. [*] *Ich gäbe was dafür, wenn ich wüsste, woran du gerade denkst. (Ein Pfennig für deine Gedanken.)*
A penny saved is a penny earned. [*] *Wer den Pfennig nicht ehrt ... (Ein gesparter Pfennig ist ein verdienter Pfennig.)*
not to have a penny to one's name *keinen Pfennig mehr in der Tasche haben* **65/66**
to cost a pretty penny *ein hübsches Sümmchen kosten*

people
Some people just have it. *Einige wissen eben, wie man's anstellt.* **80**

pick
to pick on someone *auf jn. herumhacken*
to pick up after someone *js. Dreck wegmachen* **150**

P

to pick up something *etwas aufschnappen; sich etwas angewöhnen; lernen* **121**

picture
to get the picture *die Situation richtig einschätzen; kapieren* **157**

pie
as easy as pie *kinderleicht*
to eat humble pie *Abbitte tun; zu Kreuze kriechen (Demütigungskuchen essen)*

piece
a piece of cake *das ist ein Kinderspiel, kinderleicht* **27/28/50/71**
to give someone a piece of one's mind *jm. gründlich die Meinung sagen*
to go to pieces *zusammenbrechen*

pig
to be pig-headed *dickköpfig sein* **7**
to make a pig of oneself *wie ein Schwein fressen*

pin
to pin something on someone *jm. etwas anhängen*
You could hear a pin drop. [*] *Man konnte eine Nadel fallen hören.*

pipe
Put that in your pipe and smoke it! [*] *Lass dir das gesagt sein!*

pitch
pitch black *pechschwarz* **103**
to pitch in *sein Scherflein beitragen; (Geld) zusammenlegen*

place
all over the place *überall* **111**
in the first place *erstens*
to fall into place *Sinn ergeben; den Zusammenhang klar hervortreten lassen*
to put someone in his place *jn. in seine Schranken weisen*

plan
to go according to plan *planmäßig verlaufen*

play
to play along with something *mit den Wölfen heulen; gute Miene zum bösen Spiel machen*
to play (it) safe *kein Risiko eingehen; auf Nummer Sicher gehen*

plunge
to take the plunge *den entscheidenden Schritt wagen; den Sprung ins kalte Wasser wagen*

pocket
to have someone in one's pocket *jn. in der Tasche haben; jn. kontrollieren*

point
to be beside the point *nicht zur Sache gehörig*
to come to the point *zur Sache kommen*
to make one's point *seine Ansicht klar machen/durchsetzen*
up to a point *bis zu einem gewissen Grad*
to give some pointers *ein paar Tipps geben* **27**

post
to keep someone posted *jn. auf dem Laufenden halten*

practice
Practice makes perfect. [*] *Übung macht den Meister.*
Practice what you preach. *Mach nicht nur Sprüche, sondern handele auch entsprechend.* **155**
to put something into practice *etwas in die Praxis umsetzen*

pressure
to put on the pressure *unter Druck setzen* **139**

pretty
pretty much the same thing *so ziemlich dasselbe*
to be sitting pretty *wie der Hase im Kohl; sich in einer vorteilhaften Situation befinden*

P

pride
to be someone's pride and joy *js. ganzer Stolz sein*
to swallow one's pride *seinen Stolz vergessen (runter schlucken) und sich entschuldigen*

profile
to keep a low profile *sich im Hintergrund halten*

propose
to propose to *einen Heiratsantrag machen* **155**

pull
to pull oneself together *sich zusammenreißen*
to pull something off *(Erfolg) erringen; etwas schaffen*

punches
not to pull one's punches *kein Blatt vor den Mund nehmen*

put
Put up or shut up! [*] *Akzeptier's oder halt's Maul!*
to put someone out *jm. Ungelegenheiten bereiten*
to put someone up to something *jn. zu etwas anstiften*
to put something off *etwas verschieben*
to put up with something *sich etwas gefallen lassen*

question
That's out of the question. *Das kommt nicht in Frage.*
to pop the question *einen Heiratsantrag machen*

quits
to call it quits *aufhören*

rain
rain or shine *bei jedem Wetter*
It never rains but it pours. *Ein Unglück kommt selten allein.* **87/88**

rampage
to be on a rampage *sich austoben*

rant
to rant and rave *sich nicht einkriegen vor Zorn; endlos fluchen und schimpfen*

rap
to take the rap for something *eine Sache ausbaden müssen*

rat
rat race *Karrieredruck (Rattenrennen)* **37**
to rat on someone *jn. verpfeifen*
to smell a rat *Lunte/den Braten riechen*

raw
a raw deal *unfaire Behandlung*

read
to read something into something *etwas in etwas hinein-lesen/-interpretieren*

real
the real McCoy *der wahre Jakob*

rear
to bring up the rear *die Nachhut bilden*

reason
It stands to reason that ... *es ist klar, dass ...*
There is every reason to believe that ... *Alles spricht dafür, dass ...*
to listen to reason *Vernunft annehmen*

rebound
to be on the rebound *eine gescheiterte Beziehung hinter sich haben*

record
for the record/off the record *offiziell/inoffiziell*
to set the record straight *etwas klarstellen*

red
to be in the red *rote Zahlen schreiben* **62**
to catch someone red-handed *jn. auf frischer Tat ertappen* **134**

R

rein
to give someone free rein *jm. freien Lauf lassen*
to keep a tight rein on someone *jn. fest an der Kandare haben*

reputation
to live up to one's reputation *seinem Ruf alle Ehre machen*

resort
as a last resort *wenn alle Stricke reißen; als letzte Möglichkeit*

retreat
to beat a hasty retreat *das Feld schnell räumen*

rhyme
without rhyme or reason *ohne Sinn und Verstand*

rich
to strike it rich/big *überraschend zu Geld kommen* **78**

right
It serves you right. *Das geschieht dir recht.*
to get something right *etwas richtig verstehen*
to put/set something to rights *etwas in Ordnung bringen; sauber machen*

ringer
to be a dead ringer for someone *js. Doppelgänger sein* **97**

riot
to read the riot act *ernstlich warnen*
to run riot *sich austoben*

rise
Rise and shine! [*] *Steh auf! (Erheb dich und leuchte!)* **101**

risk
to run the risk of doing something *Gefahr laufen, etwas zu tun*

robbery
daylight robbery *Nepp; die Kundschaft ausnehmen*

rocker
to be off one's rocker *übergeschnappt sein*

Rome
When in Rome, do as the Romans do. [*] *Heule mit den Wölfen. Andere Länder, andere Sitten – und nach denen sollte man sich richten.*

roof
to go through the roof *vor Wut an die Decke gehen*
to have a roof over one's head *ein Dach über dem Kopf haben*

roost
to rule the roost *das Regiment/Wort führen*

ropes
to know the ropes *sich auskennen*

rose
It's no bed of roses. *Das ist kein Honigschlecken.*

rough
to rough it *ein spartanisches Leben führen*

round
not to get round to something *nicht dazukommen, etwas zu erledigen*

rub
to rub it in *jm. etwas unter die Nase reiben*
to rub off on someone *auf jn. abfärben* **145/146**
to rub someone the wrong way *etwas tun, was jm. gegen den Strich geht*

rug
to pull the rug out from under someone *jm. den Boden unter den Füßen wegziehen*

rule
rule of thumb *Faustregel*

R

run
in the long run *auf die Dauer*
to be out of the running *keine Aussichten/Chancen haben*
to run across something *zufällig auf etwas stoßen*
to run much deeper *tiefere Ursachen haben* **100**

rut
to be in a rut *sich in eingefahrenen Gleisen bewegen; stagnieren*

sack
to hit the sack *sich (zum Schlafen) hinhauen*

safe
better safe than sorry *lieber auf Nummer Sicher gehen* **157/158**
safe and sound *heil und gesund*
There's safety in numbers. [*] *Zu mehreren ist man sicherer.*

sailing
From now on it's all plain/smooth sailing. *Von jetzt an läuft alles wie geschmiert.*

same
all the same *trotzdem*
to be all the same to someone *einem ganz Wurscht/ egal sein*

sardine
packed (in) like sardines *zusammengezwängt wie in einer Sardinenbüchse*

say
to have something to say for oneself *etwas zu seiner Rechtfertigung sagen*
What would you say to ... *Was hältst du von ...?*
You can say that again! *Das kannst du zweimal sagen!* **2**

scarce
to make oneself scarce *sich rar machen*

school
to drop out of school *vorzeitig von der Schule abgehen* **4**

score
to have a score to settle with someone *eine alte Rechnung mit jm. zu begleichen haben*

scratch
to start from scratch *ganz von vorn anfangen*

screw
to have a screw loose *eine Schraube locker haben*
to put the (thumb)screws on someone *jn. unter Druck setzen*
to screw up *Mist bauen; sich einen Patzer leisten* **118**

secrecy
to swear someone to secrecy *jn. zur Geheimhaltung verpflichten* **21**

see
Seeing is believing. [*] *Das muss man gesehen haben, um es zu glauben.*
to see about/to something *sich kümmern um*
to see somebody *mit jm. regelmäßig ausgehen* **151**
to see through someone *jn. durchschauen* **39**

seed
to go to seed *herunterkommen*

sell
to sell someone/something short *jn./etwas unterschätzen* **79/80**

sense
to come to one's senses *wieder zur Vernunft kommen*

serious
to get serious *eine feste Beziehung haben* **48**

set
to be all set (to) *bereit sein*
to set someone back *jm. Unkosten verursachen* **64**

S

settle
to settle down *sich beruhigen* **29**
to settle for something *sich mit etwas zufrieden geben*
to settle something once and for all *etwas ein fur alle Mal aus der Welt schaffen* **95**

shame
a crying shame *eine Schande*
to put someone to shame *jn. in den Schatten stellen* **35**

share
Share and share alike. [*] *Zu gleichen Teilen.*

sheep
the black sheep of the family *das schwarze Schaf der Familie* **49**

sheet
as white as a sheet *kreidebleich*
three sheets to the wind *sternhagelvoll*

shell
to come out of one's shell *aus sich herausgehen*

ship
shipshape *in tadelloser Ordnung*
to run a tight ship *ein strenges Kommando führen*

shirt
to keep one's shirt on *sich nicht aufregen*
to lose one's shirt *sein letztes Hemd verlieren*

shoe
If the shoe fits, wear it. [*] *Wer sich angesprochen fühlt, fühlt sich zu Recht angesprochen.*
Now the shoe is on the other foot. [*] *Jetzt will er plötzlich nichts mehr davon wissen.*
to be in someone's shoes *in js. Haut stecken*

shoot
Shoot! [*] *Schieß los! Sag schon!* 3

shop
to set up shop *eine Firma aufziehen; sich einrichten*
to talk shop *fachsimpeln*

short
to run short of something *etwas wird knapp*

shot
a long shot *ein kühner Versuch*
to call the shots *am längeren Hebel sitzen; eine Sache kontrollieren*

shoulder
to give someone the cold shoulder *jm. die kalte Schulter zeigen*

show
to get the show on the road *den Plan umsetzen*
to run the show *hinter der Bühne die Fäden ziehen; die Fäden in der Hand halten*
to steal the show *die Schau stehlen*

shut
to shut up *das Maul halten* **41/59**

sick
to be sick and tired of something *etwas wirklich satt haben* **40/62/107**

side
the wrong side of the tracks *aus ärmlichen Verhältnissen* **43**
to be on the safe side *um ganz sicher zu gehen*
to look on the bright side *auch die guten Seiten sehen* **105**
to take sides *Partei ergreifen*

sight
a sight for sore eyes *eine Augenweide* **141**
not to be able to stand the sight of someone *js. Anblick nicht ertragen können*
Out of sight, out of mind. [*] *Aus den Augen, aus dem Sinn.*
to lose sight of someone *jn. aus den Augen verlieren*

silver
to be born with a silver spoon in one's mouth *ein Glückskind sein*

sin
to live in sin *in wilder Ehe leben*

sink
Sink or swim. [*] *Auf Biegen und Brechen.*

size
to cut someone down to size *jn. in seine Schranken verweisen*
Try that on for size! [*] *Was sagt man denn dazu!?*

skeleton
a skeleton in the closet/cupboard *ein dunkles Geheimnis*

skin
by the skin of one's teeth *mit knapper Not*
That's no skin off my nose. [*] *Das juckt/kratzt mich nicht.*
to get under one's skin *jm. unter die Haut gehen; jm. nahe gehen*
to have a thick/thin skin *dickfellig/zartbesaitet sein*
to save one's skin *mit heiler Haut davonkommen*

sky
The sky's the limit. [*] *Nach oben sind keine Grenzen gesetzt.*

sleep
to sleep in *ausschlafen*
to sleep it off *einen Rausch ausschlafen*
to sleep on something *noch einmal darüber schlafen*

sleeve
to have something up one's sleeve *etwas in petto haben*
53/141/142

slide
to let something slide *die Dinge laufen lassen*

slip
to give someone the slip *jm. entwischen*
to slip up *Mist bauen; einen Fehler machen*

smart
a smart aleck *Neunmalkluger; Klugscheißer* **128/137**

smoke
to go up in smoke *in nichts zerrinnen; sich zerschlagen*
Where there's smoke, there's fire. [*] *Da (z. B. am Gerücht) wird wohl was dran sein. (Wo's Rauch gibt, gibt's auch Feuer.)*

snap
to snap out of something *seine Laune ändern* **93**
Make it snappy! *Mach's kurz! Geht's auch flotter?*

snowball
not to have a snowball's chance in hell *völlig ohne Chance sein*

sob
a sob-story *ein Rührstück*

sober
to sober up *ausnüchtern* **53**

sock
Put a sock in it! *Halt's Maul!*
to sock it to someone *jm. Saures geben*

soften
to soften someone up *jn. erweichen; js. Herz rühren*

sold
to be sold on something *von einer Sache überzeugt sein* **71/72**

sooner
No sooner said than done. [*] *Gesagt, getan.*
The sooner, the better. [*] *Je früher, desto besser.*

S

spade
to call a spade a spade *das Kind beim richtigen Namen nennen*

spanner
to throw a spanner/wrench in the works *jm. einen Knüppel zwischen die Beine werfen*

speak
generally speaking *allgemein*
not to be on speaking terms with someone *mit jm. nicht sprechen*
so to speak *sozusagen*
to speak too soon *den Tag vor dem Abend loben; etwas vorschnell als sicher darstellen* **115/116**

spell
to spell something out for someone *jm. etwas haarklein erklären*

spick
spick and span *blitzsauber; wie aus dem Ei gepellt* **146**

split
to split up *sich trennen* 40

spot
to have a soft spot for someone *eine Schwäche für jn. haben*
to put someone on the spot *jn. in Verlegenheit bringen*

square
to go back to square one *wieder ganz von vorn beginnen*

stab
to have a stab at something *etwas mal ausprobieren*

stake
to have a stake in *interessiert/beteiligt sein an*

standby
on standby *in Reserve*

stand
to know where one stands *wissen, woran man ist*

star
to thank one's lucky stars that *von Glück sagen können, dass*

start
for starters *für den Anfang*
to get off to a bad start *einen schlechten Start haben*
to get off to a flying start *einen fantastischen Start haben*

stay
to stay put *sich nicht vom Fleck rühren*

steam
to blow/let off steam *seinem Zorn Luft machen*
to get all steamed up *vor Wut kochen*
to run out of steam *abschlaffen; nachlassen*

steer
to steer clear of ... *... aus dem Wege gehen*

stick
a stick-in-the-mud *jemand, der keine Lust auf etwas Neues hat* **95/96**
to stick it out *durchhalten*
to stick up for someone *sich für jn. einsetzen*

stiff
to bore someone stiff *jn. zu Tode langweilen*

sting
to take the sting out of something *einer Sache die Schärfe/die Härte nehmen*

stitch
A stitch in time saves nine. [*] *Gleich getan ist viel gespart.*
stitch without a stitch on *splitternackt*

stock
to have ... in stock *... auf Lager haben* **102**

stomach
to have no stomach for something *keinen Nerv auf eine Sache haben*
to turn one's stomach *js. Magen umdrehen; jm. Ubelkeit verursachen* **55/56**

stone
A rolling stone gathers no moss. [*] *Ein rollender Stein setzt kein Moos an.*
to leave no stone unturned *nichts unversucht lassen* **91/92**

stop
to put a stop to ... *... ein Ende machen*
to stop at nothing *vor nichts zurückschrecken*
to stop dead *plötzlich aufhören*

story
the same old story *das alte Lied*
to make/cut a long story short *um es kurz zu machen*

straight
straight off *sofort*
to get something straight *etwas richtig verstehen*

strange
strangely enough *seltsamerweise*

straw
That's the last straw! *Jetzt reicht es mir aber!*
the straw that broke the camel's back *der Tropfen, der das Fass zum Überlaufen brachte* **13/14/41**

streak
to be on a winning streak *eine Glückssträhne haben*

stride
to take something (in one's) stride *etwas mühelos bewältigen*
to make great strides *große Fortschritte machen*

strike
to strike it rich *einen (finanziellen) Volltreffer landen* **78**
to strike someone as *auf jn. den Eindruck machen als* **36**

string
no strings attached *ohne Bedingungen*
to pull strings *seine Beziehungen spielen lassen*

stuck
to be stuck *festsitzen* **114**
to be stuck to *festsitzen an* **128**
to be stuck with ... *... nicht mehr loswerden können*

stuff
to know one's stuff *sich gut auskennen*

stuffing
to knock the stuffing out of someone *jn. windelweich hauen* **5**

style
to cramp one's style *jn. sich nicht recht entfalten lassen*

suck
to suck up to someone *jm. in den Hintern kriechen*

sudden
all of a sudden *plötzlich* **72/152**

summer
Indian summer *Altweibersommer*

sure
Be sure to ... *Vergiss/Vergesst nicht ...*
sure enough *tatsächlich*
to be sure of oneself *selbstsicher sein*
to make sure *um sicherzustellen*

surface
to scratch the surface *nur an der Oberfläche ritzen*

surprise
to be good for a surprise *für eine Überraschung gut sein* **40**
to take someone by surprise *jn. überrumpeln*

swear
to swear by *auf etwas schwören*

sweat
No sweat! [*] *Kein Problem!*
to sweat it out *etwas mit Hangen und Bangen durchstehen*

sweep
to make a clean sweep of *reinen Tisch machen*

swing
in full swing *in vollem Gange*

system
to get something out of one's system *etwas loswerden; sich von etwas befreien*

T
to a T *haargenau*

tab
to keep tabs on *Buch führen über; sich auf dem Laufenden halten über*

table
to turn the tables on *den Spieß umdrehen*

tail
with one's tail between one's legs *mit eingezogenem Schwanz*

take
How did he take it? *Wie hat er's aufgenommen?*
not to take something lying down *etwas nicht einfach schlucken/hinnehmen*
Take it from me. [*] *Verlass dich darauf.*
Take it or leave it. [*] *Mach, was du willst.*
to take after someone *jm. ähneln*

to take it out on someone *seinen Zorn an jm. auslassen*
to take off *abhauen* **96**
to take someone up on something *jm. beim Wort nehmen*
You can't take it with you. [*] *Du kannst es nicht mit ins Grab nehmen.*

talk
Now you're talking! [*] *Das lässt sich schon eher hören!*
to be all talk *nur Sprüche machen* **6**
to be the talk of the town *Stadtgespräch sein*
to talk back to someone *jm. eine freche Antwort geben*
to talk someone into/out of something *jm. etwas ein-/ausreden*

tell
I told you so. [*] *Ich hab's dir ja gleich gesagt.* **97**
to tell on someone *jn. verpetzen*
to tell someone off *jn. ausschimpfen*
You never can tell. [*] *Man kann nie wissen.*
You're telling me! [*] *Wem sagen Sie das!*

temper
to control one's temper *ruhig bleiben*
to lose one's temper *die Beherrschung verlieren*

terms
to come to terms with something *sich mit etwas abfinden; etwas bewältigen*

that
just like that *einfach so*

there
So there. [*] *Da hast du's.*

thick
to lay it on thick *dick auftragen; übertreiben*

thing
not to know the first thing about *keinen Deut haben von*
to be torn between one thing and another *hin- und hergerissen sein*

to know a thing or two *sich auskennen*
to make a (big) thing/deal about something *wegen etwas ein Riesentheater machen*

think
to think twice about *sich eine Sache gründlich überlegen*

thought
to have second thoughts *Zweifel bekommen; es sich doch noch anders überlegen* **148**

throat
to be at each other's throats *einen Riesenstreit haben*
to cut one's own throat *sich selbst ruinieren*
to jump down someone's throat *jn. verbal angreifen*
to ram something down someone's throat *jm. etwas aufzwingen*

thumb
to twiddle one's thumbs *Däumchen drehen; die Hände in den Schoß legen*
under one's thumb *in js. Gewalt; unter js. Fuchtel*

tight
to sit tight *sich nicht vom Fleck rühren*

time
all in good time *einer nach dem anderen; alles zu seiner Zeit.* **107/108**
for the time being *vorläufig*
It's about time! [*] *Endlich!*
Time flies when you're having fun. [*] *Die Zeit vergeht wie im Fluge, wenn man sich amüsiert.* **113/114**
to be pressed for time *unter Zeitdruck stehen*
to bide one's time *abwarten*
to have a good time *sich großartig amüsieren* **33/154**
to have a hard time *Schwierigkeiten haben* **61**
to kill time *Zeit totschlagen* **111/112**
to take one's time *sich Zeit lassen*

tip
the tip of the iceberg *die Spitze des Eisbergs* **99/100**
to be on the tip of one's tongue *einem auf der Zunge liegend, doch man kommt nicht darauf*

toe
to keep someone on his toes *jm. keinen ruhigen Moment gönnen; jn. in dauernder Bereitschaft halten* **126**

Tom
a Peeping Tom *Spanner; Voyeur*
Tom, Dick and Harry *Hinz und Kunz*

tomorrow
Never put off until tomorrow what you can do today. [*]
Was du heute kannst besorgen, das verschiebe nicht auf morgen.

tongue
with one's tongue in one's cheek *ironisch; mit Hintergedanken*

tooth
to cut one's teeth on ... *sich an ... die Zähne ausbeißen*
to have a sweet tooth *gern Süßigkeiten essen*

top
to be top of the class *Klassenbeste/r sein* **133**
to blow one's top *einen Wutanfall haben*

touch
out of touch *keinen Kontakt/Bezug haben* **127**
to keep in touch *in Verbindung bleiben*
to put on the finishing touches *den letzten Schliff geben* **116**

towel
to throw in the towel/sponge *die Flinte ins Korn werfen; das Handtuch werfen* **135/136**

T

town
to paint the town red *auf die Pauke hauen; die Puppen tanzen lassen*

track
off the beaten track *abgelegen; nicht nach dem gängigen Muster*
the wrong side of the tracks *aus ärmlichen Verhältnissen* **43**
to be on the right track *auf der richtigen Fährte sein*
to lose track of someone/something *jn./etwas aus den Augen verlieren* **115**
to track someone down *jn. aufspüren* **53**

trap
to keep one's trap shut *den Mund halten* **22**

travel
to travel through *auf der Durchreise sein* **102**

tree
to bark up the wrong tree *auf dem Holzweg sein; an der falschen Adresse sein*

trick
a trick of the trade *Profitrick; Berufsgeheimnis*
to be up to one's tricks *seine alte Schau/Nummer abziehen* **81**
to do the trick *den Zweck erfüllen*

trouble
to be asking for trouble *das Schicksal herausfordern; sich nur selbst Schwierigkeiten bereiten*
to give someone trouble *jm. Schwierigkeiten machen* **33**

turn
to take a turn for the better/worse *verbessern/verschlimmern*
to take turns *sich abwechseln*
to turn against someone *sich gegen jn. stellen*
to turn in *ins Bett gehen* **31**
to turn something down *etwas ablehnen*

twist
a twist of fate *Ironie des Schicksals; Zufall* **34**

two
to put two and two together *sich etwas zusammenreimen*
two of a kind *zwei vom gleichen Schlag*

up
to be on the up-and-up *in Ordnung/ehrlich sein*
to be up against *(einer Schwierigkeit) gegenüberstehen*
to be up to something *etwas im Schilde führen*
to feel up to *sich in der Lage fühlen zu; in Stimmung sein zu*

upstage
to upstage someone *jn. in den Hintergrund drängen*

use
It's no use. *Es ist zwecklos.* **29/30/31**

visit
to pay someone a visit *jn. besuchen* **8**

voice
at the top of one's voice *aus vollem Halse (schreien)*
to lose one's voice *die Stimme verlieren*
to raise one's voice *die Stimme erheben*

wagon
to be on the wagon *dem Alkohol abschwören*

walk
to walk all over someone *über js. Gefühle oder Rechte hinwegtrampeln*
to walk out on someone *jn. im Stich lassen*
all walks of life *alle Lebensbereiche und Gesellschaftsschichten*

wash
to come out in the wash *sich in Luft auflösen; sich von selbst regeln*

waste
to go to waste *vergeudet werden* **125**
to let something go to waste *etwas vergeuden; etwas nicht anrühren* **125**
Waste not, want not. [*] *Spare in der Zeit, so hast du in der Not.*

watch
to be on the watch/lookout for *auf der Hut sein vor*

water
like water off a duck's back *ohne den geringsten Eindruck zu machen*
Still waters run deep. [*] *Stille Wasser sind tief.*
to be in hot water *in Teufels Küche sein* **99**
water under the bridge/over the dam *vergeben und vergessen*

wavelength
to be on the same wavelength *auf der gleichen Wellenlänge liegen*

way
by the way *übrigens* **42**
to go a long way *lange vorhalten* **18**
to go out of one's way *ein Übriges tun; sich besonders anstrengen*
to have one's own way *seinen Willen durchsetzen*
to have ways *Mittel und Wege haben* **56**

weather
under the weather *sich gesundheitlich nicht wohl fühlen*

weight
to be worth its weight in gold *Gold wert sein; unbezahlbar; unschätzbar* **75**
to pull one's own weight *seinen Teil leisten/beitragen*
to throw one's weight about/around *sich breit machen; seinen Einfluss geltend machen*

welcome
to outstay/wear out one's welcome *länger bleiben, als man erwünscht ist*

well
All's well that ends well. [*] *Ende gut, alles gut.* **40**
It's just as well that ... *Es ist im Grunde schon gut so, dass ...*
That is all very well, but ... *Das ist ja alles schön und gut, aber ...*

what
to know what's what *Bescheid wissen*

while
worth one's while *der Mühe wert*

whistle
as clean as a whistle *blitzblank*
to blow the whistle on someone *jn. verpfeifen*
to wet one's whistle *etwas trinken*

win
to win someone over *jn. für sich gewinnen/auf seine Seite ziehen* **75**

wind
to get wind of something *von einer Sache Wind bekommen* **89/90**
to take the wind out of someone's sails *jm. den Wind aus den Segeln nehmen*

wing
to take someone under one's wing *jn. unter seine Fittiche nehmen; in Schutz nehmen*

wise
a wise guy *Klugscheißer*
none the wiser *nicht klüger als zuvor*
to be wise to something *Bescheid wissen über*

wish
to read every wish from someone's eyes *jm. jeden Wunsch von den Augen ablesen* **54**
wishful thinking *Wunschdenken*

W

wit
to be at one's wits' end *sich nicht mehr zu helfen wissen; mit seiner Weisheit am Ende sein*
to have one's wits about one *seine fünf Sinne beisammen haben*
to scare the wits out of someone *jn. zu Tode erschrecken*

wolf
to cry wolf *blinden Alarm schlagen; Alarm geben, um jn. aufzurütteln* **15/16**

wood/forest
not to be able to see the wood/forest for the trees *den Wald vor lauter Bäumen nicht sehen können*

wool
to pull the wool over someone's eyes *jn. hinters Licht führen*

word
not to be able to get a word in edgeways *nicht zu Wort kommen können*
not to mince one's words *kein Blatt vor den Mund nehmen*
to break/keep one's word *sein Wort brechen/halten*
to eat one's words *zurücknehmen müssen, was man gesagt hat* **33/34**
to go back on one's word *eine Zusage nicht einhalten*
to have a way with words *sich gut ausdrücken können; wortgewandt sein*
to have a word with someone *mit jm. ernsthaft reden*
to put in a good word for someone *ein gutes Wort einlegen für*
to take someone's word for it *js. Worten glauben schenken* **126**
to take the words right out of one's mouth *jm. das Wort aus dem Munde nehmen* **59/60**

work
All work and no play makes Jack a dull boy. [*] *Wer immer nur arbeitet, dreht durch.*
to do someone's dirty work *js. Dreckarbeit machen*

to work one's way up *sich hocharbeiten*
to work something out *eine Lösung finden* **151**

world
The world is my oyster. [*] *Die Welt liegt mir zu Füßen, ich kann machen, was ich will.*
to be dead to the world *tief und fest schlafen*
to think the world of someone *große Stücke von jm. halten*

worse/worst
if/when the worst comes to the worst *wenn alle Stricke reißen*
The worst is yet/still to come. [*] *Das Schlimmste/dicke Ende kommt erst noch.* **9**
to take a turn for the better/worse *verbessern/verschlimmern*

worth
for all one is worth *mit ganzer Kraft* **75/76**

wrap
to keep something under wraps *etwas unter Dach und Fach halten/geheim halten*
to wrap something up *eine Sache abschließen*

write
to see the writing on the wall *die Vorzeichen/Warnungen erkennen*
to write something off *eine Sache abschreiben/in den Wind schreiben*

yarn
to spin a yarn *eine Geschichte erzählen* **1**

years
to have plenty of years left in one *noch viele (gute) Jahre vor sich haben* **19**

yesterday
not born yesterday *nicht von gestern sein*

zero
to zero in on something *auf sein Ziel zusteuern*

Dieses Verzeichnis erfasst rund eintausend Idioms nach Themen, Situationen und Redeabsichten.

1. **Den Anfang machen, richtig loslegen und ein Ende finden**
2. **Aussehen, Erscheinungsbild, Anmutung**
3. **Beschreiben: die Welt da draußen**
4. **Bitten und danken**
5. **Gefühl und Gemüt**
6. **Geld: viel oder wenig?**
7. **Handeln im Alltag**
8. **Im Gespräch**
9. **Informationsfluss**
10. **Körper und Sinne**
11. **Menschliches**
12. **Mobilität: laufen, fahren und festsitzen**
13. **Vertrauliches: Tratsch, Klatsch und Geheimniskrämerei**
14. **Probleme: Versagen, Misserfolg und andere Problemlagen**
15. **Verstehen und Nichtverstehen**
16. **Natur und Wetter**
17. **Polizeiliches und Investigatives**
18. **Überraschungen**
19. **Zeit, planen und warten**
20. **Ziele erreichen**

Um die pralle Welt unserer Idioms unter magere zwanzig Überschriften zu packen, mussten wir das geistige Gebälk unserer Kategorien gelegentlich etwas anheben, sonst hätten wir für tausend Redewendungen fast ebenso viele Hauptüberschriften benötigt. Dennoch sind wir guter Hoffnung, dass Ihnen das thematische Verzeichnis – zusammen mit dem alphabetischen – den Zugriff auf die Redensarten, die Sie gerade suchen, ein wenig erleichtert. Ein bisschen gemogelt haben wir allerdings schon, stecken doch hinter Globalkategorien wie «Menschliches» noch weitere wunderbare Unterpunkte wie «Machtkämpfe, Mobbing und Hackordnung» oder «Spaß und Freud» samt allen dazugehörigen Wendungen.

Wenn es Ihnen beim Durchsehen der Listen seltsam erscheint, dass beispielsweise «to take someone's word for it» unter dem Eintrag «Diskutieren und Argumentieren» auftaucht, schauen Sie am besten im Text nach, wo sich das Idiom im Zusammenhang besser begreifen und bewerten lässt. Oder aber Sie bilden aus der angegebenen Form zunächst einmal einen vollständigen Satz: «Take my word for it!» (Das kannst du mir aber wirklich glauben!) passt ganz vorzüglich in jedes Streitgespräch.

Innerhalb der einzelnen Kategorien haben wir die einzelnen Ausdrücke nach Alphabet arrangiert: Dabei erhalten die Hauptwörter den Vorzug, fehlen die, sortieren wir das Verb ein. Wie im alphabetischen Register steht auch hier der Asterisk [*] für Wendungen, die sich nicht konjugieren lassen. Zudem findet sich bei einigen Ausdrücken, in Klammern angefügt, eine wortwörtliche Übertragung. Die Ziffern beziehen sich jeweils auf die Nummer des Textes, in dem das Idiom vorgestellt wird.

Den Anfang machen, richtig loslegen und ein Ende finden

to **act** up *loslegen; Schwierigkeiten machen* **85**
to get one's **act** together *in Gang kommen; etwas auf die richtige Bahn bringen*
to get down to **business** *eine Sache in Angriff nehmen* **123**
to be **done** for *erledigt sein* **16**
to get off on the wrong **foot** *einen schlechten Start haben*
to **get** something off the ground *loslegen; mit etwas beginnen*
Go ahead! *Mach doch, los geht's!* **159**
to jump the **gun** *voreilig sein; einen Fehlstart verursachen*
to turn over a new **leaf** *von neuem beginnen (ein neues Blatt aufschlagen)*
to call it **quits** *aufhören*
to bring up the **rear** *die Nachhut bilden*
to start from **scratch** *ganz von vorn anfangen*
to be all **set** (to) *bereit sein*
to get the **show** on the road *den Plan umsetzen*
to get off to a bad **start** *einen schlechten Start haben*
to get off to a flying **start** *einen fantastischen Start haben*

for **starters** *für den Anfang*
to put a **stop** to ... *... ein Ende machen*
to **stop** dead *plötzlich aufhören*
to make a clean **sweep** of *reinen Tisch machen*
in full **swing** *in vollem Gange*
to put on the finishing **touches** *den letzten Schliff geben* **116**
to **wrap** something up *eine Sache abschließen*

Aussehen, Erscheinungsbild, Anmutung

Beauty is in the eye of the beholder. [*] *Schönheit existiert (nur) im Auge des Betrachters.*
Beauty is only skin deep. [*] *Schönheit ist nur an der Oberfläche.*
You look like **death** warmed up/over. *Du siehst aus wie zwischen achtzig und scheintot.*
an ugly **duckling** *hässliches Entlein*
a **dump** *ein mieses Loch* **88/146**
to be the spitting **image** of someone *jm. wie aus dem Gesicht geschnitten sein*
like two **peas** in a pod *sich gleichen wie ein Ei dem anderen*
pitch black *pechschwarz* **103**
to be a dead **ringer** for someone *js. Doppelgänger sein* **97**
as white as a **sheet** *kreidebleich*
a **sight** for sore eyes *eine Augenweide* **141**
not to be able to stand the **sight** of someone *js. Anblick nicht ertragen können*
to lose **sight** of someone *jn. aus den Augen verlieren*
without a **stitch** on *splitternackt*
to **take** after someone *jm. ähneln*

Beschreiben: die Welt da draußen

a **change** of scenery *Tapetenwechsel* **158**
The **coast** is clear. [*] *Die Luft ist rein.*
in the **limelight** *im Rampenlicht*
lock, stock and barrel *komplett*
in the **middle** of nowhere *am Ende der Welt; in einer gottverlassenen Gegend* **114**

in **mint** condition *nagelneu*
next to nothing *fast gar nichts*
odds and ends *Krimskrams; Sammelsurium; Kleinigkeiten*
open and shut *offensichtlich*
in good working **order** *voll betriebsfähig* **85**
out of **order** *defekt*
to have a little **peace** and quiet *Ruhe haben* **42**
all over the **place** *überall* **111**
to have a **roof** over one's head *ein Dach über dem Kopf haben*
to **rough** it *ein spartanisches Leben führen*
to be in a **rut** *sich in eingefahrenen Gleisen bewegen; stagnieren*
shipshape *in tadelloser Ordnung*
not a **single** one *nicht ein Einziger*
spick and span *blitzsauber; wie aus dem Ei gepellt* **146**
Tom, Dick and Harry *Hinz und Kunz*
all **walks** of life *alle Lebensbereiche und Gesellschaftsschichten*
as clean as a **whistle** *blitzblank*

Bitten und danken

to count one's **blessings** *dankbar sein für das, was man hat*
to ask a **favor** *um einen Gefallen bitten* **155**
to give someone a (helping) **hand** *jm. helfen*
to have one's **heart** set on something *das Herz an etwas hängen* **101**
to **pass** something up *verzichten auf*
to give some **pointers** *ein paar Tipps geben* **27**
to throw one's **weight** about/around *sich breit machen; seinen Einfluss geltend machen*

Gefühl und Gemüt: von Wut bis Wahnsinn

to stab someone in the **back** *jn. hintergehen/in den Rücken fallen*
to make someone's **blood** boil *js. Blut zum Wallen bringen*
to have a **bone** to pick with someone *ein Hühnchen mit jm. zu rupfen haben*

to hit the **ceiling** *in die Luft gehen* **41**
to have a **chip** on one's shoulder *vor Zorn geladen sein*
to get hot under the **collar** *wütend werden*
to **egg** someone on *anstacheln, aufhetzen*
to go off the deep **end** *ausrasten*
to get **even** with someone *es jm. heimzahlen*
to ruffle someone's **feathers** *jn. vergrätzen, verärgern* **3/4/37**
to be **fed** up with something *etwas satt haben* **10**
to pick a **fight** *Streit suchen* **7**
to **gang** up on someone *sich zusammenrotten gegen*
to get someone's **goat** *jn. auf die Palme bringen*
to go against someone's **grain** *jm. gegen den Strich gehen*
to hate someone's **guts** *jn. inbrünstig hassen*
to raise a **hand** against *die Hand erheben gegen* **5**
to fly off the **handle** *die Fassung verlieren; fuchsteufelswild werden* **129/130**
to **have** it in for someone *es auf jn. abgesehen haben*
to let someone **have** it *jm. eine Abreibung verpassen*
to blow to high **heaven** *in die Luft blasen/sprengen* **110**
All **hell** broke loose. [*] *Die Hölle war los.*
to add **insult** to injury *Wer den Schaden hat, braucht für den Spott nicht zu sorgen. (zur Verletzung auch noch die Beleidigung hinzufügen)* **34**
to stew in one's own **juice** *im eigenen Saft schmoren*
It's a **jungle** out there. *Das draußen geht's wüst zu.* **2**
to be out of one's **mind** *übergeschnappt sein* **28/70/131**
to lose one's **mind** *seinen Verstand verlieren* **101**
to be **nuts** *total verrückt sein* **39/156**
to go to **pieces** *zusammenbrechen*
to be on a **rampage** *sich austoben*
to **rant** and rave *sich nicht einkriegen vor Zorn; endlos fluchen und schimpfen*
It serves you **right**. *Das geschieht dir recht.*
to run **riot** *sich austoben*
to be off one's **rocker** *übergeschnappt sein*
to go through the **roof** *vor Wut an die Decke gehen*
to have a **score** to settle with someone *eine alte Rechnung mit jm. zu begleichen haben*
to have a **screw** loose *eine Schraube locker haben*
to come to one's **senses** *wieder zur Vernunft kommen*

to **settle** down *sich beruhigen* **29**
to keep one's **shirt** on *sich nicht aufregen*
to get under one's **skin** *jm. unter die Haut gehen; jm. nahe gehen*
to **snap** out of something *seine Laune ändern* **93**
a **sob**-story *ein Rührstück*
to blow/let off **steam** *seinem Zorn Luft machen*
to run out of **steam** *abschlaffen; nachlassen*
to get all **steamed** up *vor Wut kochen*
That's the last **straw**! *Jetzt reicht es mir aber!*
the **straw** that broke the camel's back *der Tropfen, der das Fass zum Überlaufen brachte* **13/14/41**
to turn the **tables** on *den Spieß umdrehen*
to **take** it out on someone *seinen Zorn an jm. auslassen*
to control one's **temper** *ruhig bleiben*
to lose one's **temper** *die Beherrschung verlieren*
to be at each other's **throats** *einen Riesenstreit haben*
to blow one's **top** *einen Wutanfall haben*

Gefühl und Gemüt: Liebe, Lust und Larmoyanz

Absence makes the heart grow fonder. [*] *Mit der Entfernung wächst die Sehnsucht.*
to welcome someone with open **arms** *jn. mit offenen Armen willkommen heißen* **49**
from the **bottom** of one's heart *von ganzem Herzen*
to **check** someone out *sich jn. mal genauer anschauen* **2/158**
to sweep someone off his/her **feet** *js. Herz im Sturm erobern*
to twist/wrap someone around one's little **finger** *jn. um den Finger wickeln*
to **fool** around with *rummachen mit* **28/36**
to **grow** on someone *jm. ans Herz wachsen* **71**
head over heels in love *bis über beide Ohren verliebt* **3/47/48**
My **heart** is not in it. *Ich bin nicht mit ganzem Herzen dabei.*
to steal someone's **heart** *js. Herz stehlen* **15**
to be **involved** with someone *mit jm. eine Beziehung haben* **83**
Who's the **lucky** person? *Wer ist denn die Glückliche?* **145**

in the heat of the **moment** *im Eifer des Gefechts*
on the spur of the **moment** *ohne Überlegung; spontan*
to **move** in with someone *zu jm. in die Wohnung ziehen* **144**
to sow one's wild **oats** *sich die Hörner abstoßen, über die Stränge schlagen* **83/84**
to make a **pass** at someone *einer Person gegenüber zudringlich werden; jn. anmachen*
to **propose** to *einen Heiratsantrag machen* **155**
to pop the **question** *einen Heiratsantrag machen*
to be on the **rebound** *eine gescheiterte Beziehung hinter sich haben*
to **see** somebody *mit jm. regelmäßig ausgehen* **151**
to get **serious** *eine feste Beziehung haben* **48**
to live in **sin** *in wilder Ehe leben*
to **soften** someone up *jn. erweichen; js. Herz rühren*
to **split** up *sich trennen* **40**
to have a soft **spot** for someone *eine Schwäche für jn. haben*
to be **stuck** with ... *... nicht mehr loswerden können*
a Peeping **Tom** *Spanner; Voyeur*
to **walk** out on someone *jn. im Stich lassen*
to read every **wish** from someone's eyes *jm. jeden Wunsch von den Augen ablesen* **54**

Gefühl und Gemüt: zwischen Gleichgültigkeit und Akzeptanz

not to give a **damn** *sich einen Dreck drum scheren* **151/152**
to go in one **ear** and out the other *rein ins eine Ohr, raus aus dem anderen*
What the **hell**! [*] *Was soll's?*
nothing to write **home** about *nichts besonders Großartiges*
to put something on **ice** *etwas auf Eis legen*
to **laugh** something off *etwas mit einem Lachen abtun*
to go through the **motions** *etwas völlig lustlos betreiben* **143/144**
to keep one's **options** open *nach allen Seiten offen bleiben; sich nicht festlegen*
rule of thumb *Faustregel*
to be all the **same** to someone *einem ganz Wurscht/egal sein*

Now the **shoe** is on the other foot. [*] *Jetzt will er plötzlich nichts mehr davon wissen.*
Out of **sight**, out of mind. [*] *Aus den Augen, aus dem Sinn.*
to let something **slide** *die Dinge laufen lassen*
Take it or leave it. [*] *Mach, was du willst.*
to come to **terms** with something *sich mit etwas abfinden; etwas bewältigen*
to sit **tight** *sich nicht vom Fleck rühren*
to feel **up** to *sich in der Lage fühlen zu; in Stimmung sein zu*
to come out in the **wash** *sich in Luft auflösen; sich von selbst regeln*
like **water** off a duck's back *ohne den geringsten Eindruck zu machen*

Gefühl und Gemüt: (keine) Angst

to sweat **blood** *Blut und Wasser schwitzen*
to have **butterflies** in one's stomach *nervös sein*
the **creeps** *Gruseln; Gänsehaut* **153/154**
to be on **edge** *angespannt sein* **32**
not to bat an **eye**lid *nicht mal mit der Wimper zucken*
to get cold **feet** *kalte Füße kriegen* **36**
to have **guts** *Mut haben (Därme haben)* **139**
not to have the **heart** to do something *nicht den Mut haben, etwas zu tun*
to give one the **jitters** *jn. nervös machen* **6**
to be scared out of one's **mind** *völlig verängstigt sein; Panik kriegen*
to have the **nerve** to do something *den Mut/die Frechheit besitzen, etwas zu tun*
to wet one's **pants** *sich in die Hosen machen*
to have no **stomach** for something *keinen Nerv auf eine Sache haben*
to **stop** at nothing *vor nichts zurückschrecken*
to **sweat** it out *etwas mit Hangen und Bangen durchstehen*
with one's **tail** between one's legs *mit eingezogenem Schwanz*
to scare the **wits** out of someone *jn. zu Tode erschrecken*

Geld: viel oder wenig?

to cost an **arm** and a leg *ein Heidengeld kosten* **67/159**
to tighten one's **belt** *den Gürtel enger schnallen*
to be a little short on **cash** *ein bisschen knapp bei Kasse sein* **42**
not to have a red **cent** *keinen roten Heller besitzen* **65**
to **check** something out *etwas prüfen; etwas ausleihen* **142**
to save something for a rainy **day** *etwas auf die hohe Kante legen*
Easy come, easy go. [*] *Wie gewonnen, so zerronnen.*
to make **ends** meet *finanziell über die Runden kommen* **40/61/62**
to break **even** *ohne Gewinn oder Verlust abschließen; die Gewinnzone erreichen*
to live from **hand** to mouth *von der Hand in den Mund leben*
to burn a **hole** in someone's pocket *(Geld) ausgeben wollen*
to eat someone out of **house** and home *jm. die Haare vom Kopf fressen* **61**
There's ... **in** it for you. *Du kannst dir ... dazuverdienen.* **87**
to work for one's **keep** *für Kost und Logis arbeiten; sich bezahlt machen* **60**
to make a **killing** *ein Haufen Geld verdienen*
to cut one's **losses** *seine Verluste begrenzen*
to **make** do with something *mit etwas auskommen*
to make a **mint** *einen Haufen Geld verdienen*
Money doesn't grow on trees. [*] *Geld wächst nicht auf Bäumen.*
Money is no object. [*] *Geld spielt keine Rolle.* **77/78**
to get one's **money**'s worth *etwas für sein Geld bekommen*
to have **money** to burn *Geld wie Heu haben*
to put one's **money** where one's mouth is *den Worten (finanzielle) Taten folgen lassen* **73/74**
to throw **money** out of the window *Geld zum Fenster rausschmeißen* **80**
to pay through the **nose** *einen Haufen Geld blechen*
A **penny** saved is a penny earned. [*] *Wer den Pfennig nicht ehrt ... (Ein gesparter Pfennig ist ein verdienter Pfennig.)*
not to have a **penny** to one's name *keinen Pfennig mehr in der Tasche haben* **65/66**
to cost a pretty **penny** *ein hübsches Sümmchen kosten*

to **pitch** in *sein Scherflein beitragen; (Geld) zusammenlegen*
to strike it **rich**/big *überraschend zu Geld kommen* **78**
to **set** someone back *jm. Unkosten verursachen* **64**
to lose one's **shirt** *sein letztes Hemd verlieren*
the wrong **side** of the tracks *aus ärmlichen Verhältnissen* **43**
The **sky**'s the limit. [*] *Nach oben sind keine Grenzen gesetzt.*
A **stitch** in time saves nine. [*] *Gleich getan ist viel gespart.*
to **strike** it rich *einen (finanziellen) Volltreffer landen* **78**
Waste not, want not. [*] *Spare in der Zeit, so hast du in der Not.*
to be worth its **weight** in gold *Gold wert sein; unbezahlbar; unschätzbar* **75**

Handeln im Alltag: arbeiten – oder auch nicht

to **bend** over backwards *sich ein Bein ausreißen (um jn. zufrieden zu stellen)*
to earn one's daily **bread** *sein täglich Brot verdienen* **15**
Business before pleasure. [*] *Erst die Arbeit, dann das Vergnügen.*
to be in **charge** *verantwortlich sein* **152**
to cut **corners** *etwas beschleunigen, indem man es nachlässiger ausführt*
to **fiddle** around with *rummachen mit*
not to lift a **finger** *keinen Finger krumm machen*
to work one's **fingers** to the bone *sich kaputtarbeiten* **62**
to **get** away from it all *sich (auf die Insel) absetzen*
to have one's **hands** full *alle Hände voll zu tun haben* **126**
to bring **home** the bacon *die Brötchen nach Hause bringen; den Lebensunterhalt verdienen* **35/36/40**
to sign on the dotted **line** *Vertrag unterschreiben*
to burn the **midnight** oil *bis tief in die Nacht arbeiten* **101/102**
to keep one's **nose** to the grindstone *sich schinden; schuften*
to put one through one's **paces** *jn./etwas auf seine Belastbarkeit testen* **11/12**
not up to **par**/below par *keine Konkurrenz darstellen*
to put something into **practice** *etwas in die Praxis umsetzen*
rat race *Karrieredruck (Rattenrennen)* **37**

a **raw** deal *unfaire Behandlung*
to be in the **red** *rote Zahlen schreiben* **62**
to put/set something to **rights** *etwas in Ordnung bringen; sauber machen*
not to get **round** to something *nicht dazukommen, etwas zu erledigen*
to drop out of **school** *vorzeitig von der Schule abgehen* **4**
to set up **shop** *eine Firma aufziehen; sich einrichten*
to have ... in **stock** ... *auf Lager haben* **102**
to pull **strings** *seine Beziehungen spielen lassen*
to twiddle one's **thumbs** *Däumchen drehen; die Hände in den Schoß legen*
to be **top** of the class *Klassenbeste/r sein* **133**
a **trick** of the trade *Profitrick; Berufsgeheimnis*
to take **turns** *sich abwechseln*
to go out of one's **way** *ein Übriges tun; sich besonders anstrengen*
to pull one's own **weight** *seinen Teil leisten/beitragen*
worth one's **while** *der Mühe wert*
All **work** and no play makes Jack a dull boy. [*] *Wer immer nur arbeitet, dreht durch.*
to do someone's dirty **work** *js. Dreckarbeit machen*
to **work** one's way up *sich hocharbeiten*

Handeln im Alltag: Entscheidungen treffen, Risiken eingehen

to cross a **bridge** when one comes to it *alles zu seiner Zeit (die Brücke überqueren, wenn man bei ihr ankommt)*
to take the **bull** by the horns *den Stier bei den Hörnern packen* **9/10**
to eat one's **cake** and have it too *man kann nicht alles haben, man muss sich entscheiden* **23/24**
to take a **chance** *etwas riskieren* **50/78**
to put all one's **eggs** in one basket *alles auf eine Karte setzen*
to put an **end** to *beenden; kurzen Prozess machen* **75/89**
to play with **fire** *mit dem Feuer spielen*
to have a **go** *einen Versuch machen/wagen*
to meet someone **halfway** *einen Kompromiss treffen*

to try one's **hand** at something *sein Glück mit etwas versuchen*
to let someone be the **judge** *jn. selbst bewerten/entscheiden lassen* **61**
to take one's **life** in one's own hands *sein Leben aufs Spiel setzen*
to be out on a **limb** *sich in einer gefährlichen Lage befinden*
to push one's **luck** *sein Schicksal herausfordern*
to try one's **luck** at ... *sein Glück mit ... versuchen* **49**
to make up one's **mind** *einen Entschluss fassen*
to risk one's **neck** *Kopf und Kragen riskieren*
to stick one's **neck** out *für jn. den Kopf hinhalten*
a golden **opportunity** *eine gute Gelegenheit*
to take **pains** *sich Mühe geben*
to **play** (it) safe *kein Risiko eingehen; auf Nummer Sicher gehen*
to take the **plunge** *den entscheidenden Schritt wagen; den Sprung ins kalte Wasser wagen*
as a last **resort** *wenn alle Stricke reißen; als letzte Möglichkeit*
to beat a hasty **retreat** *das Feld schnell räumen*
to run the **risk** of doing something *Gefahr laufen, etwas zu tun*
to **run** across something *zufällig auf etwas stoßen*
a long **shot** *ein kühner Versuch*
by the **skin** of one's teeth *mit knapper Not*
not to have a **snowball**'s chance in hell *völlig ohne Chance sein*
to have a **stab** at something *etwas mal aus probieren*
to have a **stake** in *interessiert/beteiligt sein an*
to leave no **stone** unturned *nichts unversucht lassen* **91/92**
to be torn between one **thing** and another *hin- und hergerissen sein*
to **think** twice about *sich eine Sache gründlich überlegen*
to have second **thoughts** *Zweifel bekommen; es sich doch noch anders überlegen* **148**
to **work** something out *eine Lösung finden* **151**

Im Gespräch: ablehnen und negativ bewerten

The **advantages** outweigh the disadvantages. *Die Vorteile überwiegen die Nachteile.* **56**
to keep at **arm's** length *auf Abstand halten*
to get off someone's **back** *jn. in Ruhe lassen*
to get out of **bed** on the wrong side *auf dem falschen Fuß aufstehen*
to take the **biscuit**/to take the cake *der letzte Heuler sein*
Over my dead **body**. [*] *Nur über meine Leiche.*
to nip something in the **bud** *etwas im Keim ersticken* **81/82**
not to be **cut** out for something *nicht dazu geschaffen sein*
to **cut** it out *aufhören mit*
not to be worth a **damn** *keinen Pfifferling wert sein*
not to be one's **day** *einen schlechten Tag haben* **117/118**
That'll be the **day**! [*] *Nie im Leben! Das ist äußerst unwahrscheinlich.* **105/106**
The **disadvantages** outweigh the advantages. *Die Nachteile überwiegen die Vorteile.* **56**
a **drop** in the bucket/ocean *ein Tropfen auf dem heißen Stein*
to be wet behind the **ears** *noch nicht trocken hinter den Ohren sein*
Easier said than done. [*] *Leichter gesagt als getan.*
to be **fishy** *einem Spanisch vorkommen*
not to do much **good** *nicht viel nützen* **21**
to turn in one's **grave** *sich im Grab umdrehen*
to **grin** and bear it *gute Miene zum bösen Spiel machen*
to split **hairs** *Haarspalterei betreiben*
to **have** had it *etwas satt haben* **10/112**
to have a change of **heart** *die Meinung ändern*
Wild **horses** would not make me do it! *Keine zehn Pferde würden mich dazu bringen!*
Knock it off! *Schluss damit!* **139**
to treat someone like a **leper** *jn. wie einen Aussätzigen behandeln* **131**
There's no **love** lost between them. *Sie haben nichts für einander übrig.*
by all/no **means** *auf jeden/keinen Fall*
to change one's **mind** *es sich anders überlegen*
nit-picking *kleinliche Korinthenkackerei (Nissen suchen)*
No way/go! [*] *Niemals!* **28/39/67**

Nothing doing! [*] *Das kommt gar nicht in Frage!*
That's out of the **question**. *Das kommt nicht in Frage.*
a crying **shame** *eine Schande*
to be **sick** and tired of something *etwas wirklich satt haben* **40/62/107**
to be all **talk** *nur Sprüche machen* **6**
to **turn** something down *etwas ablehnen*
to take the **wind** out of someone's sails *jm. den Wind aus den Segeln nehmen*

Im Gespräch: argumentieren und diskutieren

to give a straight **answer** *ohne Umschweife antworten* **94**
to have made one's **bed** and have to lie in it *die Suppe, die man sich eingebrockt hat, auslöffeln müssen*
to be all for the **best** *wirklich gar nicht so schlimm sein* **32/40**
The early **bird** catches the worm. [*] *Morgenstund' hat Gold im Mund.*
a **blessing** in disguise *Glück im Unglück*
a mixed **blessing** *ein zweischneidiges Schwert; eine zweischneidige Sache* **147/148**
to beat around/about the **bush** *nicht zur Sache kommen; wie die Katze um den heißen Brei herumschleichen* **93/94/110/153**
to put one's **cards** on the table *die Karten auf den Tisch legen*
to be the **case** *zutreffen; der Fall sein* **91**
to come out of the **closet** *sich selbst offen zu etwas bekennen; sich «outen»* **155**
Join the **club**! [*] *Jetzt hat's dich auch erwischt, willkommen im Club!*
when it **comes** to ... *was ... angeht/betrifft* **42**
to be **concerned** about *sich Sorgen machen um* **48**
to be **dead** set on something *sich auf etwas versteifen*
to run much **deeper** *tiefere Ursachen haben* **100**
to play it by **ear** *improvisieren*
to see **eye** to eye with someone *mit jm. übereinstimmen*
by **far** *bei weitem* **56**
So **far**, so good. [*] *So weit, so gut.*
That **figures**. [*] *Das sieht ihm ähnlich; das ist genau, was ich erwartet habe.*

to **go** over something *etwas durchsprechen* **27**
it **goes** without saying that *es ist selbstverständlich, dass*
with a **grain** of a salt *unter Vorbehalt*
to take for **granted** *als selbstverständlich betrachten*
to **harp** on something *herumreiten auf etwas*
to draw the **line** *die Grenze ziehen; Halt machen*
to read between the **lines** *zwischen den Zeilen lesen*
a **matter** of opinion *Geschmackssache/Anschauungssache*
if my **memory** serves me right *wenn ich mich richtig erinnere*
to refresh one's **memory** *sein Gedächtnis auffrischen*
not to **mention** *ganz zu schweigen von*
to cross one's **mind** *jm. in den Sinn kommen*
to have someone/something in **mind** *schon wissen, wer/was* **149**
to keep an open **mind** *sich anderer Leute Vorschläge und Ideen vorbehaltlos anhören*
to slip one's **mind** *aus dem Gedächtnis entgleiten; entfallen*
to speak one's **mind** *aus seinem Herzen keine Mördergrube machen; Klartext reden*
to face the **music** *die Suppe auslöffeln*
to hit the **nail** on the head *den Nagel auf den Kopf treffen* **123/124**
to get down to the **nitty**-gritty *die eigentliche Sache anpacken*
to be beside the **point** *nicht zur Sache gehörig*
to come to the **point** *zur Sache kommen*
to make one's **point** *seine Ansicht klar machen/durchsetzen*
up to a **point** *bis zu einem gewissen Grad*
pretty much the same thing *so ziemlich dasselbe*
not to pull one's **punches** *kein Blatt vor den Mund nehmen*
to **read** something into something *etwas in etwas hineinlesen/-interpretieren*
the **real** McCoy *der wahre Jakob*
It stands to **reason** that ... *es ist klar, dass ...*
There is every **reason** to believe that ... *Alles spricht dafür, dass ...*
to listen to **reason** *Vernunft annehmen*
all the **same** *trotzdem*
What would you **say** to ...? *Was hältst du von ...?*
You can **say** that again! *Das kannst du zweimal sagen!* **2**
Shoot! [*] *Schieß los! Sag schon!* **3**
to talk **shop** *fachsimpeln*

to take **sides** *Partei ergreifen*
That's no **skin** off my nose. [*] *Das juckt/kratzt mich nicht.*
Put a **sock** in it! *Halt's Maul!*
to be **sold** on something *von einer Sache überzeugt sein* **71/72**
to call a **spade** a spade *das Kind beim richtigen Namen nennen*
so to **speak** *sozusagen*
generally **speaking** *allgemein*
the same old **story** *das alte Lied*
to make/cut a long **story** short *um es kurz zu machen*
strangely enough *seltsamerweise*
no **strings** attached *ohne Bedingungen*
sure enough *tatsächlich*
to **swear** by *auf etwas schwören*
to a **T** *haargenau*
to **talk** back to someone *jm. eine freche Antwort geben*
Now you're **talking**! [*] *Das lässt sich schon eher hören!*
You're **telling** me! [*] *Wem sagen Sie das!*
just like **that** *einfach so*
So **there**. [*] *Da hast du's.*
to lay it on **thick** *dick auftragen; übertreiben*
to be on the **tip** of one's tongue *einem auf der Zunge liegend, doch man kommt nicht darauf*
to keep one's **trap** shut *den Mund halten* **22**
by the **way** *übrigens* **42**
It's just as **well** that ... *Es ist im Grunde schon gut so, dass ...*
That is all very **well**, but ... *Das ist ja alles schön und gut, aber ...*
not to be able to get a **word** in edgeways *nicht zu Wort kommen können*
to break/keep one's **word** *sein Wort brechen/halten*
to go back on one's **word** *eine Zusage nicht einhalten*
to have a **word** with someone *mit jm. ernsthaft reden*
to take someone's **word** for it *js. Worten glauben schenken* **126**
not to mince one's **words** *kein Blatt vor dem Mund nehmen*
to eat one's **words** *zurücknehmen müssen, was man gesagt hat* **33/34**
to spin a **yarn** *eine Geschichte erzählen* **1**

Im Gespräch: bestätigen, betonen und hervorheben

to hit the **bull**'s eye *den Nagel auf den Kopf treffen*
That's the way the **cookie** crumbles. [*] *Da liegt der Hase im Pfeffer; so sieht's aus.*
to make a big **deal** about something *wegen etwas ein Riesentheater machen* **139**
Just what the **doctor** ordered *genau, was man braucht*
You can't teach an old **dog** new tricks. [*] *Was Hänschen nicht lernt, lernt Hans nimmermehr.* **19/20**
to keep one's **fingers** crossed *jm. die Daumen drücken* **49/50**
I would like to be a **fly** on the wall. *Dort möchte ich Mäuschen sein.*
to put one's **foot** down *einen festen Standpunkt einnehmen; seine Meinung klar machen* **138**
to make a **fuss** over *Theater machen wegen; sich übertriebene Umstände machen*
to stop in **midstream** *mitten in einer Tätigkeit (beim Sprechen) innehalten*
to stick out a **mile** *ganz offensichtlich sein*
There's **nothing** to it. [*] *Das ist kinderleicht.*
out of the **ordinary** *etwas Ungewöhnliches*
to go **overboard** *übertreiben* **71**
to **overdo** it *überbeanspruchen; übertreiben*
A **penny** for your thoughts. [*] *Ich gäbe was dafür, wenn ich wüsste, woran du gerade denkst. (Ein Pfennig für deine Gedanken.)*
as easy as **pie** *kinderleicht*
a **piece** of cake *das ist ein Kinderspiel, kinderleicht* **27/28/50/71**
Seeing is believing. [*] *Das muss man gesehen haben, um es zu glauben.*
Share and share alike. [*] *Zu gleichen Teilen.*
If the **shoe** fits, wear it. [*] *Wer sich angesprochen fühlt, fühlt sich zu Recht angesprochen.*
to make a (big) **thing**/deal about something *wegen etwas ein Riesentheater machen*
to take the **words** right out of one's mouth *jm. das Wort aus dem Munde nehmen* **59/60**

Im Gespräch: aufmuntern, ermutigen und Hoffnung machen

Almost there! [*] *Gleich haben wir's!* **116**
to have the **ball** in one's court *am Zug sein*
Cheer up! [*] *Sei nicht so verbissen!* **105/156**
to keep one's **chin** up *die Ohren steif halten*
Every **cloud** has a silver lining. [*] *Jedes Unglück hat auch seine guten Seiten.*
come **hell** or high water *egal, welche Schwierigkeiten auch überwunden werden müssen* **97/98**
to **keep** at it/it up *weitermachen; nicht aufgeben*
The **least** I can do. *Das Mindeste, was ich tun kann.* **114**
Lightning never strikes in the same place twice. *Ungewöhnliche Unfälle wiederholen sich nicht. (Der Blitz schlägt nie zweimal an derselben Stelle ein.)*
to keep a stiff upper **lip** *die Ohren steif halten; sich nicht entmutigen lassen* **57/58**
to have the **makings** of ... *das Zeug zu ... haben*
Every **man** for himself. [*] *Jeder kämpft für sich allein.*
to cry over spilled **milk** *passiert ist passiert, hin ist hin* **12/29/30**
to put someone's **mind** at rest *jn. beruhigen*
to take one's **mind** off *jn. auf andere Gedanken bringen* **1**
That was **par** for the course. *Damit hatten wir schon gerechnet.*
Practice makes perfect. [*] *Übung macht den Meister.*
It never **rains** but it pours. *Ein Unglück kommt selten allein.* **87/88**
to **see** about/to something *sich kümmern um*
to look on the bright **side** *auch die guten Seiten sehen* **105**
Sink or swim. [*] *Auf Biegen und Brechen.*
to **stick** it out *durchhalten*
No **sweat**! [*] *Kein Problem!*
to **talk** someone into/out of something *jm. etwas ein-/ausreden*
to put in a good **word** for someone *ein gutes Wort einlegen für*

Im Gespräch: ermahnen und warnen

Beggars can't be choosers. [*] *Du kannst es dir nicht leisten, wählerisch zu sein.*
not to judge a **book** by its cover *nicht aufgrund von Außerlichkeiten urteilen, der Schein könnte trügen.* **137/138**
Give me a **break**! [*] *Jetzt mach mal halblang!* **4**
to waste one's **breath** *unnütz Worte machen*
to mean **business** *es wirklich ernst meinen* **6**
to mind one's own **business** *sich um seine eigenen Angelegenheiten kümmern* **63/64**
When the **cat**'s away, the mice will play. [*] *Wenn die Katze aus dem Haus ist, tanzen die Mäuse auf dem Tisch.*
to count one's **chickens** before they hatch *das Fell des Bären verkaufen, ehe man ihn hat*
Curiosity killed the cat. [*] *Sei nicht so neugierig. (Die Neugierde tötete die Katze.)*
Let sleeping **dogs** lie. [*] *Schlafende Hunde soll man nicht wecken.* **7/8**
to go **easy** on someone *nicht so streng mit jm. sein*
or **else** *oder es passiert was* **6**
to keep an **eye** on something *auf etwas aufpassen*
to keep one's **eyes** peeled *die Augen offen halten; genau beobachten*
to be on one's **guard** *auf der Hut sein*
to go to someone's **head** *jm. zu Kopfe steigen*
to keep a cool **head** *einen kühlen Kopf bewahren* **130**
You can lead a **horse** to water but you can't make it drink. [*] *Man kann jn. nur ermutigen, handeln muss er aber schließlich selbst. (Du kannst ein Pferd ans Wasser führen, aber es nicht zum Trinken zwingen.)*
Hold your **horses**! *Immer mit der Ruhe!*
to **let**/leave well enough alone *was gut genug ist, nicht weiter verbessern*
If you don't like it, you can **lump** it. *Wenn dir's nicht passt, kannst du's ja bleiben lassen.*
to poke one's **nose** into something *seine Nase in etwas stecken*
to pour **oil** on troubled waters *die Gemüter beruhigen (Öl auf stürmisches Wasser gießen)*
to read the **riot** act *ernstlich warnen*

When in **Rome**, do as the Romans do. [*] *Heule mit den Wölfen. Andere Länder, andere Sitten – und nach denen sollte man sich richten.*
It's no bed of **roses**. *Das ist kein Honigschlecken.*
better **safe** than sorry *lieber auf Nummer Sicher gehen* **157/158**
There's **safety** in numbers. [*] *Zu mehreren ist man sicherer.*
to **sell** someone/something short *jn./etwas unterschätzen* **79/80**
to be on the safe **side** *um ganz sicher zu gehen*
Be **sure** to ... *Vergiss/Vergesst nicht ...*
to make **sure** *um sicherzustellen*
You can't **take** it with you. [*] *Du kannst es nicht mit ins Grab nehmen.*
I **told** you so. [*] *Ich hab's dir ja gleich gesagt.* **97**
the **tip** of the iceberg *die Spitze des Eisbergs* **99/100**
be on the **watch**/lookout for *auf der Hut sein vor*
to see the **writing** on the wall *die Vorzeichen/Warnungen erkennen*

Im Gespräch: kritisieren und beschuldigen

to have **bats** in the belfry *einen Vogel haben*
not fit to hold a **candle** to *jm. nicht das Wasser reichen können*
This isn't all it's **cracked** up to be. *Es ist nicht so gut, wie alle gesagt haben.*
to have seen better **days** *bessere Zeiten gesehen haben*
to leave much to be **desired** *viel zu wünschen übrig lassen*
to point the **finger** at *jm. die Schuld geben*
to wash one's **hands** of something *seine Hände in Unschuld waschen*
to bite someone's **head** off *jn. ausschimpfen*
a lousy **job** *äußerst dürftige Leistung* **120**
to take someone down a **peg** *jn. auf seine normale Größe zurechtstutzen*
to **pick** on someone *auf jn. herumhacken*
to give someone a **piece** of one's mind *jm. gründlich die Meinung sagen*

Put that in your **pipe** and smoke it! [*] *Lass dir das gesagt sein!*
to put someone in his **place** *jn. in seine Schranken weisen*
Practice what you preach. *Mach nicht nur Sprüche, sondern handele auch entsprechend.* **155**
Put up or shut up! [*] *Akzeptier's oder halt's Maul!*
without **rhyme** or reason *ohne Sinn und Verstand*
to **rub** it in *jm. etwas unter die Nase reiben*
to cut someone down to **size** *jn. in seine Schranken verweisen*
to **tell** someone off *jn. ausschimpfen*
to jump down someone's **throat** *jn. verbal angreifen*

Im Gespräch: kontrastieren und vergleichen

to take a **backseat** to *die zweite Geige spielen*
to go from **bad** to worse *noch schlechter werden*
as blind as a **bat** *blind wie eine Fledermaus* **129**
a **chip** off the old block *ganz der Vater sein* **121/122**
to spread like wild**fire** *sich wie ein Lauffeuer verbreiten*
There's plenty more **fish** in the sea. [*] *Es gibt noch viele andere Möglichkeiten.*
as **good** as new *so gut wie neu* **120**
to be half as **good** as *auch nur halb so gut sein wie* **147**
The **grass** is always greener on the other side (of the fence). [*] *Was man bereits hat, ist nie gut genug. (Auf der anderen Seite des Zauns ist das Gras immer grüner.)*
Give him an **inch** and he'll take a mile. *Wenn man jm. den kleinen Finger gibt, wird gleich die ganze Hand genommen.*
to **inch** closer to *näher rücken an* **9**
This isn't **like** you. *Das sieht dir aber überhaupt nicht ähnlich.* **141**
the **likes** of *so etwas wie; solche wie*
Great **minds** think alike. [*] *Große Geister denken gleich.*
as if I had fallen off the **moon** *als wäre ich vom Mond gefallen* **22**
to make a **mountain** out of a molehill *aus einer Mücke einen Elefanten machen*
like **night** and day *(unterschiedlich) wie Tag und Nacht* **3**
to **pass** as *durchgehen als*

to throw **pearls** before the swine *Perlen vor die Säue werfen*
like two **peas** in a pod *sich wie ein Ei dem anderen gleichen*
to be on the same **wavelength** *auf der gleichen Wellenlänge liegen*

Im Gespräch: Schmeichelei, Lob und Verehrung

to **butter** someone up *jm. Honig ums Maul schmieren* **39/40**
Good for you. *Schön für dich. Gut gemacht.* **38**
a **pat** on the back *Lob (Schulterklopfen)*
to put someone on a **pedestal** *jn. auf ein Podest erheben*
Some **people** just have it. *Einige wissen eben, wie man's anstellt.* **80**
to have a way with **words** *sich gut ausdrücken können; wortgewandt sein*
to think the **world** of someone *große Stücke von jm. halten*

Informationsfluss

No **news** is good news. [*] *Wenn man nichts von einem hört, so heißt das, dass es ihm gut geht. (Keine Neuigkeiten sind gute Neuigkeiten.)*
That's **news** to me. *Das ist mir neu.*
to break the **news** *eine (meist traurige) Nachricht mitteilen* **51**
in a **nutshell** *in aller Kürze*
in the first **place** *erstens*
to keep someone **posted** *jn. auf dem Laufenden halten*
for the **record**/off the record *offiziell/inoffiziell*
to set the **record** straight *etwas klarstellen*
to scratch the **surface** *nur an der Oberfläche ritzen*
to keep **tabs** on *Buch führen über; sich auf dem Laufenden halten über*
How did he **take** it? *Wie hat er's aufgenommen?*
Take it from me. [*] *Verlass dich darauf.*
to **take** someone up on something *jm. beim Wort nehmen*

Körper und Sinne: Fortbewegung

to make a **beeline** for *auf etwas zustürzen*
to **catch** up with someone *jn. einholen* **13/117**
to **clear** out *sich dünnmachen* **139**
to **keel** over *plötzlich umfallen (kentern)*
to stretch one's **legs** *sich die Beine vertreten* **109**
to **take** off *abhauen* **96**

Körper und Sinne: Gesundheit, Krankheit, Tod

to be eaten **alive** *bei lebendigem Leibe gefressen werden* **14/105**
to have to go to the **bathroom** *aufs Klo müssen* **107**
to kick the **bucket** *sterben; den Löffel aus der Hand legen* **127/128**
to bite the **dust** *ins Gras beißen*
as fit as a **fiddle** *kerngesund* **101**
to zip one's **fly** *den Hosenlatz schließen* **22**
to have one **foot** in the grave *mit einem Bein im Grab stehen*
to have a **frog** in one's throat *einen Frosch im Hals haben*
a **guinea** pig *Versuchskaninchen (Meerschweinchen)*
to pump someone full of **lead** *jn. umlegen* **10**
It's a matter of **life** and death. *Es geht um Leben oder Tod.* **155**
to go into **mourning** *trauern* **15**
to **pass** away *verscheiden; sterben*
safe and sound *heil und gesund*
to turn one's **stomach** *js. Magen umdrehen; jm. Übelkeit verursachen* **55/56**
under the **weather** *sich gesundheitlich nicht wohl fühlen*

Körper und Sinne: riechen und essen

to whet one's **appetite** for something *auf den Geschmack kommen; js. Appetit auf etwas wecken*
to stink to high **heaven** *zum Himmel stinken*
to make a **pig** of oneself *wie ein Schwein fressen*
to have a sweet **tooth** *gern Süßigkeiten essen*

Körper und Sinne: schlafen

to hit the **hay** *sich aufs Ohr legen*
sleepy **head** *Schlafmütze* **101**
to sleep like a **log** *tief und fest schlafen*
to drop one's **pants** *die Hosen runterlassen* **93**
Rise and shine! [*] *Steh auf! (Erheb dich und leuchte!)* **101**
to hit the **sack** *sich (zum Schlafen) hinhauen*
to **sleep** in *ausschlafen*
to **sleep** it off *einen Rausch ausschlafen*
to **sleep** on something *noch einmal darüber schlafen*
to **turn** in *ins Bett gehen* **31**
to be dead to the **world** *tief und fest schlafen*

Körper und Sinne: sehen

to lay **eyes** on ... ... *betrachten* **135**
to catch a **glimpse** of *einen flüchtigen Blick erhaschen von* **76**
not to give someone a second **look** *jn. keines zweiten Blickes würdigen* **135**
to get a closer **look** *sich etwas aus der Nähe anschauen*
to **look** someone up and down *jn. genau inspizieren*
to give someone the **once**-over *jn. kurz mustern*
to take a **peek** *einen Blick werfen* **48**

Körper und Sinne: sprechen und hören

at the top of one's **lungs** *aus vollem Halse (schreien)* **38**
You could hear a **pin** drop. [*] *Man konnte eine Nadel fallen hören.*
at the top of one's **voice** *aus vollem Halse (schreien)*
to lose one's **voice** *die Stimme verlieren*
to raise one's **voice** *die Stimme erheben*

Körper und Sinne: trinken

to hit the **bottle** *saufen* **55**
to **drown** one's sorrows *seinen Kummer im Alkohol ertränken*

to drink like a **fish** *saufen*
three **sheets** to the wind *sternhagelvoll*
to **sober** up *ausnüchtern* **53**
to be on the **wagon** *dem Alkohol abschwören*
to wet one's **whistle** *etwas trinken*

Menschliches: Charakterbeschreibungen und -leistungen

His **bark** is worse than his bite. [*] *Hunde, die bellen, beißen nicht.* **5/6**
to hit below the **belt** *unter die Gürtellinie schlagen*
to give someone the **benefit** of the doubt *den vorhandenen Zweifel zu js. Gunsten auslegen*
Birds of a feather flock together. [*] *Gleich und gleich gesellt sich gern.*
Blood is thicker than water. [*] *Gegenüber den Blutsverwandten loyal sein. (Blut ist dicker als Wasser.)*
to bite the **bullet** *die Zähne zusammenbeißen; etwas durchstehen; tapfer sein* **139/140**
to show oneself in one's true **colors** *sein wahres Gesicht zeigen*
to treat someone as an **equal** *jn. wie seinesgleichen behandeln* **47**
to set an **example** *ein Vorbild sein*
to stand on one's own two **feet** *auf eigenen Füßen stehen*
one's own **flesh** and blood *js. eigen Fleisch und Blut* **5**
He wouldn't hurt a **fly**. *Er würde keiner Fliege etwas zuleide tun.* **138**
to get a **grip** on oneself *sich zusammenreißen*
to have a good **head** on one's shoulders *ein kluger Kopf sein*
to have one's **heart** in the right place *das Herz am rechten Fleck tragen*
to dig in one's **heels** *nicht von der Stelle weichen; auf etwas beharren*
to **hit** it off *sich auf Anhieb gut verstehen*
a **jack**-of-all-trades *Hansdampf in allen Gassen*
to hide one's **light** under a bushel *js. Licht unter den Scheffel stellen*
This isn't **like** you. *Das sieht dir aber überhaupt nicht ähnlich.* **141**

to step out of **line** *aus der Rolle fallen; seine Grenzen überschreiten*
a **man** after one's own heart *ein Mann ganz nach seinem/ihrem Geschmack* **10**
to have a one-track **mind** *immer nur dasselbe (Sex!) im Kopf haben*
as hard as **nails** *eisern; unbarmherzig*
to be **pig**-headed *dickköpfig sein* **7**
to be someone's **pride** and joy *js. ganzer Stolz sein*
to swallow one's **pride** *seinen Stolz vergessen (runterschlucken) und sich entschuldigen*
to keep a low **profile** *sich im Hintergrund halten*
to **pull** oneself together *sich zusammenreißen*
to **put** someone out *jm. Ungelegenheiten bereiten*
to **rub** off on someone *auf jn. abfärben* **145/146**
to make oneself **scarce** *sich rar machen*
the black **sheep** of the family *das schwarze Schaf der Familie* **49**
to come out of one's **shell** *aus sich herausgehen*
to have a thick/thin **skin** *dickfellig/zartbesaitet sein*
to be **sure** of oneself *selbstsicher sein*
not to **take** something lying down *etwas nicht einfach schlucken/hinnehmen*
to be on the **up**-and-up *in Ordnung/ehrlich sein*
water under the bridge/over the dam *vergeben und vergessen*
Still **waters** run deep. [*] *Stille Wasser sind tief.*
to take someone under one's **wing** *jn. unter seine Fittiche nehmen; in Schutz nehmen*
wishful thinking *Wunschdenken*
to have one's **wits** about one *seine fünf Sinne beisammen haben*
for all one is **worth** *mit ganzer Kraft* **75/76**

Menschliches: Machtkämpfe, Mobbing und Hackordnung

to have an **axe/ax** to grind *eigennützige Zwecke verfolgen (eine Axt zu schärfen haben)*
at someone's **beck** and call *jm. auf den leisesten Wink gehorchen*

to make/poke **fun** of someone *sich über jm. lustig machen*
to play **games** with *mit jm. sein Spielchen treiben* **89**
to give someone **hell** *jn. fertig machen*
to **kick** oneself *sich in den Hintern beißen*
to **kill** someone *jn. fertig machen* **7**
to bring someone to his **knees** *jn. in die Knie zwingen*
to **knuckle** under *nachgeben; sich einer stärkeren Macht unterwerfen* **53/54**
to pull someone's **leg** *jn. einen Bären aufbinden; jn. veräppeln* **51/52/102**
to make someone's **life** miserable *jm. das Leben vermiesen* **10**
to meet one's **match** *seinen Meister finden*
to be at the **mercy** of someone *jm. auf Gedeih und Verderb ausgeliefert sein*
to make **mincemeat** of someone *aus jm. Hackfleisch machen*
to breathe down someone's **neck** *jm. im Nacken sitzen* **8**
to lead someone by the **nose** *jn. völlig kontrollieren*
to have someone in the **palm** of one's hand *jn. in der Hand haben*
to wear the **pants** in one's house *zu Hause die Hosen anhaben* **95**
to eat humble **pie** *Abbitte tun; zu Kreuze kriechen (Demütigungskuchen essen)*
to have someone in one's **pocket** *jn. in der Tasche haben; jn. kontrollieren*
to put on the **pressure** *unter Druck setzen* **139**
to **put** up with something *sich etwas gefallen lassen*
to give someone free **rein** *jm. freien Lauf lassen*
to keep a tight **rein** on someone *jn. fest an der Kandare haben*
to rule the **roost** *das Regiment/Wort führen*
to put the (thumb)**screws** on someone *jn. unter Druck setzen*
to put someone to **shame** *jn. in den Schatten stellen* **35**
to run a tight **ship** *ein strenges Kommando führen*
to call the **shots** *am längeren Hebel sitzen; eine Sache kontrollieren*
to run the **show** *hinter der Bühne die Fäden ziehen; die Fäden in der Hand halten*
to steal the **show** *die Schau stehlen*
to **sock** it to someone *jm. Saures geben*

to take the **sting** out of something *einer Sache die Schärfe/die Härte nehmen*
to cramp one's **style** *jn. sich nicht recht entfalten lassen*
to ram something down someone's **throat** *jm. etwas aufzwingen*
under one's **thumb** *in js. Gewalt; unter js. Fuchtel*
to keep someone on his **toes** *jm. keinen ruhigen Moment gönnen; jn. in dauernder Bereitschaft halten* **126**
with one's **tongue** in one's cheek *ironisch; mit Hintergedanken*
to **upstage** someone *jn. in den Hintergrund drängen*
to **walk** all over someone *über js. Gefühle oder Rechte hinwegtrampeln*
to have one's own **way** *seinen Willen durchsetzen*
to have **ways** *Mittel und Wege haben* **56**

Menschliches: Sozialkontakte pflegen und aufgeben

to jump on the **bandwagon** *mit den Wölfen heulen*
to **bump**/run into someone *jn. zufällig treffen*
to keep someone **company** *jm. Gesellschaft leisten*
Two's **company**, three's a crowd. [*] *Drei sind einer zu viel.* **160**
Three's a **crowd**. [*] *Drei sind einer zu viel.* **160**
to be all **ears** *ganz Ohr sein*
to rub **elbows**/shoulders *am gleichen Ort sein, in Kontakt kommen* **45/46/47**
to follow in someone's **foot**steps *in js. Fußstapfen treten* **49**
Be my **guest**. [*] *Bedien dich; nimm dir, was du brauchst.* **114/159/160**
to make oneself at **home** *es sich bequem machen*
to **play** along with something *mit den Wölfen heulen; gute Miene zum bösen Spiel machen*
No **sooner** said than done. [*] *Gesagt, getan.*
to **stick** up for someone *sich für jn. einsetzen*
to keep in **touch** *in Verbindung bleiben*
to pay someone a **visit** *jn. besuchen* **8**
to outstay/wear out one's **welcome** *länger bleiben, als man erwünscht ist*

Menschliches: Spaß und Freud

to have a **ball** *sich köstlich amüsieren*
to be on **cloud** nine *im siebten Himmel sein*
to be one's **cup** of tea *js. Berufung/Lieblingsbeschäftigung sein; jm. liegen* **37/38**
a **cut** above *besser als alles andere*
to make one's **day** *jn. glücklich machen; js. Tag retten* **103/104**
to be no **fun** to be around someone *keinen Spaß machen, mit jm. zusammen zu sein* **152**
to be **happy** for someone *sich für jn. freuen* **145**
to have one's **head** in the clouds *im siebten Himmel sein*
in seventh **heaven** *im siebten Himmel* **145**
just for the **hell** of it *nur zum Spaß; aus Jux und Tollerei* **155/156**
for **kicks** *zum Spaß*
to **lead** someone on *falsche Hoffnungen wecken*
to take/get a **load** off one's mind *jm. eine Last von der Seele nehmen*
to have a good **time** *sich großartig amüsieren* **33/154**
to paint the **town** red *auf die Pauke hauen; die Puppen tanzen lassen*
All's **well** that ends well. [*] *Ende gut, alles gut.* **40**

Menschliches: unangenehme Zeitgenossen und deren Eigenschaften

to take **advantage** of someone *jn. übervorteilen/ausnutzen* **149/150**
to twist someone's **arm** *jn. zwingen*
pompous **ass** *arroganter Arsch; aufgeblasener Kerl*
butterfingers *ungeschickte Person; Tollpatsch*
not to let someone hear the **end** of this *jm. keine Ruhe mehr geben; etwas immer wieder erwähnen* **131**
to make a **fool** of someone/oneself *sich zum Narren machen*
He thinks he is God's **gift** to women. *Was seine Wirkung auf Frauen angeht, ist er sehr von sich eingenommen. (Er denkt, er sei Gottes Geschenk an die Frauen.)*
a **good**-for-nothing *Taugenichts* **44**

to be up to no **good** *etwas im Schilde führen*
a/one **heck**/hell of a ... *ein Wahnsinns...* **19**
who the **heck**/hell *wer zum Teufel* **89**
to get on someone's **nerves** *jm. auf die Nerven gehen* **25/148/152**
to look down one's **nose** at *jn. verachten; auf jn. herabschauen* **43/44**
to turn up one's **nose** at something *die Nase über etwas rümpfen*
a **pain** in the ass/neck *eine Nervensäge* **41/42**
to live up to one's **reputation** *seinem Ruf alle Ehre machen*
to **rub** someone the wrong way *etwas tun, was jm. gegen den Strich geht*
to pull the **rug** out from under someone *jm. den Boden unter den Füßen wegziehen*
to give someone the cold **shoulder** *jm. die kalte Schulter zeigen*
a **smart** aleck *Neunmalkluger; Klugscheißer* **128/137**
not to be on **speaking** terms with someone *mit jm. nicht sprechen*
to **steer** clear of ... *... aus dem Wege gehen*
a **stick**-in-the-mud *jemand, der keine Lust auf etwas Neues hat* **95/96**
to bore someone **stiff** *jn. zu Tode langweilen*
to knock the **stuffing** out of someone *jn. windelweich hauen* **5**
to **suck** up to someone *jm. in den Hintern kriechen*
to be up to one's **tricks** *seine alte Schau/Nummer abziehen* **81**
to give someone **trouble** *jm. Schwierigkeiten machen* **33**
to **turn** against someone *sich gegen jn. stellen*
two of a kind *zwei vom gleichen Schlag*
a **wise** guy *Klugscheißer*

Mobilität: laufen, fahren und festsitzen

to be on the **go** *auf Achse sein*
to **head** for ... *Richtung ... fahren* **13/109**
like greased **lightning** *wie ein geölter Blitz*
to **make** it to ... *es bis nach ... schaffen* **13**
to get a **move** on *einen Zahn zulegen; sich beeilen*

to follow one's **nose** *immer der Nase nach gehen*
packed (in) like **sardines** *zusammengezwängt wie in einer Sardinenbüchse*
to **stay** put *sich nicht vom Fleck rühren*
A rolling **stone** gathers no moss. [*] *Ein rollender Stein setzt kein Moos an.*
to be **stuck** *festsitzen* **114**
to be **stuck** to *festsitzen an* **128**
off the beaten **track** *abgelegen; nicht nach dem gängigen Muster*
to **travel** through *auf der Durchreise sein* **102**

Vertrauliches: Tratsch, Klatsch und Geheimniskrämerei

to spill the **beans** *ein Geheimnis preisgeben* **21/22/91**
This is just **between** you and me. *Das bleibt unter uns.*
to get something off one's **chest** *sich etwas von der Seele schaffen* **153**
through/from the **grapevine** *vom Hörensagen; durch Gerüchte*
to keep something under one's **hat** *etwas für sich behalten*
straight from the **horse**'s mouth *etwas brühwarm erzählt bekommen; etwas aus erster Hand erfahren* **17/18**
hush money *Schmiergeld*
to **hush** something up *etwas unter den Tisch kehren*
to be skating on thin **ice** *ein heikles Thema anschneiden/besprechen*
to be **in** on something *eingeweiht sein in*
to **keep** something to oneself *etwas für sich behalten* **44**
to blow the **lid** off something *(z. B. einen Skandal) aufdecken*
to play **lip**-service to something *ein Lippenbekenntnis ablegen zu etwas*
to have a big **mouth** *ein Klatschmaul haben* **24**
to shoot one's **mouth** off *blöd quatschen*
to keep one's **nose** clean *sich aus etwas heraushalten*
to rub someone's **nose** in it *jn. mit der Nase auf etwas stoßen; jn. an etwas erinnern*
to **pick** up something *etwas aufschnappen; sich etwas angewöhnen; lernen* **121**
to swear someone to **secrecy** *jn. zur Geheimhaltung verpflichten* **21**

a **skeleton** in the closet/cupboard *ein dunkles Geheimnis*
Where there's **smoke**, there's fire. [*] *Da (z. B. am Gerücht) wird wohl was dran sein. (Wo's Rauch gibt, gibt's auch Feuer.)*
to get something out of one's **system** *etwas loswerden; sich von etwas befreien*
to be the **talk** of the town *Stadtgespräch sein*
to **tell** on someone *jn. verpetzen*
to get **wind** of something *von einer Sache Wind bekommen* **89/90**
to keep something under **wraps** *etwas unter Dach und Fach halten/geheim halten*

Probleme: Versagen, Misserfolg und andere Problemlagen

to **bite** off more than one can chew *mehr in Angriff nehmen, als man bewältigen kann* **31/32**
the **blind** leading the blind *Unbedarfte, die anderen Unbedarften etwas erklären; hoffnungsloser Versuch*
to burn the **candle** at both ends *die eigenen Kräfte überfordern*
to build **castles** in the air *Luftschlösser bauen* **45**
Too many **cooks** spoil the broth/soup. [*] *Viele Köche verderben den Brei.*
to be up the **creek** (without a paddle) *in Schwierigkeiten stecken, ohne dass sich eine Lösung anbietet* **85/86**
to lead a **dog**'s life *ein Hundeleben führen*
to go to the **dogs** *vor die Hunde gehen*
to go **downhill** *den Bach runtergehen; versacken; sich verschlimmern* **150**
down the **drain** *den Bach runtergehen* **131/132**
to go back to the **drawing** board *wieder von vorn beginnen*
up to one's **ears** *bis über beide Ohren*
to have **egg** on one's face *ins Fettnäpfchen treten*
to play second **fiddle** (to someone) *die zweite Geige spielen (nach jm.)*
to put one's **foot** in one's mouth/it *ins Fettnäpfchen treten*
There **goes** my ...! *Mein ... ist futsch!* **30**
to bite the **hand** that feeds one *den Ast absägen, auf dem man sitzt*

to get out of **hand** *außer Kontrolle geraten* **22/151**
to go **haywire** *durcheinander geraten*
to be over someone's **head** *js. Fähigkeiten übersteigen; jn. überfordern*
to go down**hill** *den Bach runtergehen; versacken; sich verschlimmern* **150**
no **laughing** matter *nichts, was man auf die leichte Schulter nehmen könnte*
to be on one's last **legs** *aus dem letzten Loch pfeifen*
to be in up to one's **neck** in *bis über beide Ohren in etwas stecken*
like looking for a **needle** in a haystack *als ob man eine Nadel im Heuhaufen sucht* **125/126**
to **pick** up after someone *js. Dreck wegmachen* **150**
to take the **rap** for something *eine Sache ausbaden müssen*
to be out of the **running** *keine Aussichten/Chancen haben*
to **screw** up *Mist bauen; sich einen Patzer leisten* **118**
to go to **seed** *herunterkommen*
to **settle** for something *sich mit etwas zufrieden geben*
to be in someone's **shoes** *in js. Haut stecken*
to run **short** of something *etwas wird knapp*
to **slip** up *Mist bauen; einen Fehler machen*
to go up in **smoke** *in nichts zerrinnen; sich zerschlagen*
to throw a **spanner**/wrench in the works *jm. einen Knüppel zwischen die Beine werfen*
to **speak** too soon *den Tag vor dem Abend loben; etwas vorschnell als sicher darstellen* **115/116**
to put someone on the **spot** *jn. in Verlegenheit bringen*
to go back to **square** one *wieder ganz von vorn beginnen*
to cut one's own **throat** *sich selbst ruinieren*
to have a hard **time** *Schwierigkeiten haben* **61**
to cut one's **teeth** on ... *sich an ... die Zähne ausbeißen*
to throw in the **towel**/sponge *die Flinte ins Korn werfen; das Handtuch werfen* **135/136**
to be asking for **trouble** *das Schicksal herausfordern; sich nur selbst Schwierigkeiten bereiten*
a **twist** of fate *Ironie des Schicksals; Zufall* **34**
to be **up** against *(einer Schwierigkeit) gegenüberstehen*
It's no **use**. *Es ist zwecklos.* **29/30/31**
to go to **waste** *vergeudet werden* **125**

to let something go to **waste** *etwas vergeuden; etwas nicht anrühren* **125**
to be in hot **water** *in Teufels Küche sein* **99**
to be at one's **wits**' end *sich nicht mehr zu helfen wissen; mit seiner Weisheit am Ende sein*
to take a turn for the better/**worse** *verbessern/verschlimmern*
if/when the **worst** comes to the worst *wenn alle Stricke reißen*
The **worst** is yet/still to come. [*] *Das Schlimmste/dicke Ende kommt erst noch.* **9**
to **write** something off *eine Sache abschreiben/in den Wind schreiben*

Verstehen und Nichtverstehen

to rack one's **brains** *sich den Kopf zerbrechen*
not to have a **clue** *keine Ahnung haben*
to jump to **conclusions** *voreilige Schlüsse ziehen* **86**
to **dawn** on someone *etwas dämmert einem; jm. geht ein Licht auf* **22**
to get the **drift** *verstehen, worauf jemand hinauswill*
to be **driving** at *hinauswollen auf*
There's more to that than meets the **eye**. [*] *Es gibt mehr, als man mit bloßem Auge sehen kann.*
to **figure** something out *etwas verstehen* **24**
I don't **follow** you. *Ich kann dir nicht ganz folgen.* **147**
I **get** it! *Jetzt kapiere ich's!* **96**
What's **going** on? *Was geht denn hier vor?* **141**
It's all **Greek** to me. *Ich verstehe nur Bahnhof.*
not to be able to make **head** or tail of *aus etwas nicht schlau werden können*
off the top of one's **head** *ohne viel zu überlegen*
to put our **heads** together *die Köpfe zusammenstecken*
by **heart** *auswendig*
to get/take the **hint** *den zarten Hinweis verstehen* **139**
to do one's **homework** *sich gut vorbereiten*
not to have the faintest **idea** *nicht die leiseste Ahnung haben* **97**
to be under the **impression** that *den Eindruck haben, dass*
for all I **know** *soweit ich weiß*

to **know** something backwards/inside out *etwas in- und auswendig kennen*
You never **know**. *Man weiß ja nie (..., was noch alles möglich ist.)*
to go to any **lengths** *alles Erdenkliche tun*
to get the **message** *etwas kapieren*
in one's right **mind** *bei klarem Verstand; im Vollbesitz seiner geistigen Kräfte* **52**
to get the **picture** *die Situation richtig einschätzen; kapieren* **157**
to fall into **place** *Sinn ergeben; den Zusammenhang klar hervortreten lassen*
to get something **right** *etwas richtig verstehen*
to know the **ropes** *sich auskennen*
to **see** through someone *jn. durchschauen* **39**
to **spell** something out for someone *jm. etwas haarklein erklären*
to know where one **stands** *wissen, woran man ist*
to get something **straight** *etwas richtig verstehen*
to **strike** someone as *auf jn. den Eindruck machen als* **36**
to know one's **stuff** *sich gut auskennen*
You never can **tell**. [*] *Man kann nie wissen.*
not to know the first **thing** about *keinen Deut haben von*
to know a **thing** or two *sich auskennen*
out of **touch** *keinen Kontakt/Bezug haben* **127**
to put **two** and two together *sich etwas zusammenreimen*
to know **what**'s what *Bescheid wissen*
to be **wise** to something *Bescheid wissen über*
none the **wiser** *nicht klüger als zuvor*
not to be able to see the **wood**/forest for the trees *den Wald vor lauter Bäumen nicht sehen können*
not born **yesterday** *nicht von gestern sein*

Natur und Wetter

to rain **cats** and dogs *in Strömen gießen* **117**
rain or shine *bei jedem Wetter*
Indian **summer** *Altweibersommer*

to catch someone in the **act** *jn. auf frischer Tat ertappen*
to call someone's **bluff** *jn. auffordern, es doch zu tun; jn. auffliegen lassen*
to **catch** someone red-handed *jn. auf frischer Tat ertappen* **134**
to **crack** down on *scharf vorgehen gegen* **77**
to give (someone) the third **degree** *jn. ins Kreuzverhör nehmen* **128**
to get/let someone off the **hook** *jn. loseisen/laufen lassen* **138**
not to have a **leg** to stand on *keinerlei Beweise haben*
to shed **light** on something *Licht werfen auf*
under **lock** and key *hinter Schloss und Riegel*
to get into **mischief** *etwas «anstellen»* **122**
to get away with **murder** *ohne Strafe davonkommen*
to grease someone's **palm** *jn. bestechen (die Handfläche schmieren)* **18**
to be caught with one's **pants** down *auf frischer Tat ertappt werden*
to **pass** off as *sich ausgeben als*
to disturb the **peace** *öffentliches Ärgernis erregen* **18**
to **pin** something on someone *jm. etwas anhängen*
to **put** someone up to something *jn. zu etwas anstiften*
to **rat** on someone *jn. verpfeifen*
to smell a **rat** *Lunte/den Braten riechen*
to catch someone **red**-handed *jn. auf frischer Tat ertappen* **134**
daylight **robbery** *Nepp; die Kundschaft ausnehmen*
to have something to **say** for oneself *etwas zu seiner Rechtfertigung sagen*
to go **scot**-free *ungeschoren davonkommen* **138**
to have something up one's **sleeve** *etwas in petto haben* **53/141/142**
to give someone the **slip** *jm. entwischen*
to be on the right **track** *auf der richtigen Fährte sein*
to lose **track** of someone/something *jn./etwas aus den Augen verlieren* **115**
to **track** someone down *jn. aufspüren* **53**
to bark up the wrong **tree** *auf dem Holzweg sein; an der falschen Adresse sein*

to be **up** to something *etwas im Schilde führen*
to blow the **whistle** on someone *jn. verpfeifen*
to cry **wolf** *blinden Alarm schlagen; Alarm geben, um jn. aufzurütteln* **15/16**
to pull the **wool** over someone's eyes *jn. hinters Licht führen*

Überraschungen

to drop a **bombshell** *eine Nachricht, die wie eine Bombe einschlägt, verkünden* **34**
to let the **cat** out of the bag *die Katze aus dem Sack lassen*
not to be able to believe one's **eyes**/ears *seinen Augen/Ohren nicht trauen* **33**
My **heart** stood still. *Mir stand das Herz still.* **47**
Try that on for **size**! [*] *Was sagt man denn dazu!?*
on **standby** *in Reserve*
to be good for a **surprise** *für eine Überraschung gut sein* **40**
to take someone by **surprise** *jn. überrumpeln*

Zeit, planen und warten

out of the **blue** *aus heiterem Himmel*
That was a close **call**. *Das was aber knapp.*
like **clockwork** *wie am Schnürchen*
to call it a **day** *für heute Schluss machen*
Those were the **days**. [*] *Das waren noch Zeiten.*
to be **dying** to *kaum erwarten können* **123**
when **hell** freezes over *nie und nimmer* **119/120**
over the **hill** *die besten Jahre hinter sich habend*
an ungodly **hour** *unchristlich frühe Stunde* **117**
after **hours** *nach Geschäftsschluss* **55**
in a **jiffy** *im Nu*
at **last** *endlich* **74**
to last a **lifetime** *genug für ein ganzes Leben sein* **20**
as quick as **lightning** *blitzschnell*
once in a blue **moon** *alle Jubeljahre einmal*
in the **nick** of time *keine Sekunde zu spät; gerade noch rechtzeitig* **109/110**
to make a **night** of it *sich die Nacht um die Ohren schlagen*

to go according to **plan** *planmäßig verlaufen*
to **put** something off *etwas verschieben*
in the long **run** *auf die Dauer*
Make it **snappy**! *Mach's kurz! Geht's auch flotter?*
The **sooner,** the better. [*] *Je früher, desto besser.*
straight off *sofort*
all of a **sudden** *plötzlich* **72/152**
all in good **time** *einer nach dem anderen; alles zu seiner Zeit* **107/108**
for the **time** being *vorläufig*
It's about **time**! [*] *Endlich!*
Time flies when you're having fun. [*] *Die Zeit vergeht wie im Fluge, wenn man sich amüsiert.* **113/114**
to be pressed for **time** *unter Zeitdruck stehen*
to bide one's **time** *abwarten*
to kill **time** *Zeit totschlagen* **111/112**
to take one's **time** *sich Zeit lassen*
Never put off until **tomorrow** what you can do today. [*] *Was du heute kannst besorgen, das verschiebe nicht auf morgen.*
to go a long **way** *lange vorhalten* **18**
year in, year out *jahrein, jahraus*
to have plenty of **years** left in one *noch viele (gute) Jahre vor sich haben* **19**

Ziele erreichen: Leistung, Erfolg und Glück

to kill two **birds** with one stone *zwei Fliegen mit einer Klappe schlagen* **1/2/149**
to **cash** in on something *von etwas profitieren*
with flying **colors** *mit fliegenden Fahnen; erfolgreich*
the **cream** of the crop *der/das Allerbeste, allererste Sahne* **25/26**
to give someone a **dose** of his own medicine *jn. mit seinen eigenen Waffen schlagen* **100**
to be on one's **feet** again *wieder auf den Beinen sein; alles abgeklärt haben* **13**
Finders, keepers. [*] *Was man gefunden hat, darf man behalten.*
to have green **fingers**/a green thumb *ein Händchen für Pflanzen haben*

to have at one's **fingertips** *in Reichweite/parat haben*
at one **go** *auf einen Schlag; mit nur einem Versuch*
to make the **grade** *Erfolg haben; einen bestimmten Standard erreichen*
to come to **grips** with *mit etwas zurechtkommen; etwas in den Griff kriegen*
to hold/stand one's **ground** *sich behaupten*
single-**hand**ed *ohne fremde Hilfe*
to **handle** something *etwas schaffen* **27/31**
hands down *mit links; ohne Anstrengung*
to get one's **hands** on *etwas in die Finger kriegen* **130**
to win **hands** down *ohne Anstrengung gewinnen*
to come in **handy** *gelegen kommen*
to get the **hang**/swing of something *etwas in den Griff kriegen*
to **have** what it takes *geeignet sein*
to keep one's **head** above water *den Kopf über Wasser halten*
to hit the **jackpot** *das große Los ziehen; Riesenerfolg haben* **69/70**
Knock on/touch wood! [*] *Toi, toi, toi!*
to win by a **landslide** *mit überwältigender Mehrheit gewinnen*
to have the last **laugh** *am Ende doch noch triumphieren (den letzten Lacher haben)*
one's **lucky** day *js. Glückstag*
to be plain **lucky** *einfach nur Glück gehabt haben* **70**
to make one's **mark** *einen bleibenden Eindruck hinterlassen*
to be a **match** for someone *jm. gewachsen sein*
to make the **most** of something *das Beste aus etwas herausholen*
to hold one's **own** *sich behaupten*
to be sitting **pretty** *wie der Hase im Kohl; sich in einer vorteilhaften Situation befinden*
to **pull** something off *(Erfolg) erringen; etwas schaffen*
From now on it's all plain/smooth **sailing**. *Von jetzt an läuft alles wie geschmiert.*
to **settle** something once and for all *etwas ein für alle Mal aus der Welt schaffen* **95**
to be born with a **silver** spoon in one's mouth *ein Glückskind sein*

to save one's **skin** *mit heiler Haut davonkommen*
to thank one's lucky **stars** that *von Glück sagen können, dass*
to be on a winning **streak** *eine Glückssträhne haben*
to take something (in one's) **stride** *etwas mühelos bewältigen*
to make great **strides** *große Fortschritte machen*
to do the **trick** *den Zweck erfüllen*
to **win** someone over *jn. für sich gewinnen/auf seine Seite ziehen* **75**
The **world** is my oyster. [*] *Die Welt liegt mir zu Füßen, ich kann machen, was ich will.*
to take a turn for the better/**worse** *verbessern/verschlimmern*
to **zero** in on something *auf sein Ziel zusteuern*

Ziele erreichen: verhandeln

in the **bag** *unter Dach und Fach haben* **133/134**
to drive a hard **bargain** *mit harten Bandagen kämpfen; knallhart verhandeln* **131**
to strike a **bargain** *etwas aushandeln; eine Abmachung treffen* **67/68**
to get more than one **bargained** for *mehr als erwartet bekommen* **124**
to play one's **cards** right *klug (ver)handeln*
to stick to one's **guns** *nicht nachgeben*
to look a gift **horse** in the mouth *einem geschenkten Gaul ins Maul schauen*
at **liberty** to do something *etwas tun dürfen*
to **make** up for something *etwas wieder gutmachen*

INDEX

Die Ziffer hinter dem deutschen Stichwort verweist auf die Nummer des englischen Textes im Hauptteil, nicht auf die Seitenzahl.

A

B

D

E

H

I

J

K

L

M

N

O

P

R

W

Z